A Woman Adorned

A Woman Adorned

The Fruit of the Spirit

Wanda L. Wilson

A WOMAN ADORNED
THE FRUIT OF THE SPIRIT

iUniverse books may be ordered through booksellers or by contacting:

iUniverse
1663 Liberty Drive
Bloomington, IN 47403
www.iuniverse.com
1-800-Authors (1-800-288-4677)

Scripture quotations marked KJV are from the Holy Bible, King James Version (Authorized Version). First published in 1611. Quoted from the KJV Classic Reference Bible, Copyright © 1983 by The Zondervan Corporation.

ISBN: 978-1-4917-9742-6 (sc)
ISBN: 978-1-4917-9741-9 (e)

Library of Congress Control Number: 2016907856

Print information available on the last page.

iUniverse rev. date: 09/26/2016

For Shelby Mae, my first grandbaby girl, and her mother, Alicia; for Mia Grace and Naomi Hope (twin girls), who were born during the writing of this book, and their mother, Lindsay. May your lives be adorned with the fruit of the Spirit so that others may see Jesus in you!

"Israelite King Solomon once observed: *"He who finds a wife finds a good thing, and obtains favor from the Lord."* (Prov. 18:22). Certainly these words became true in the life of Evangelist Johnny Wilson when he met and married a beautiful lady named Wanda, thus obtaining great favor from God!

Throughout the years Wanda has been a perfect helpmeet for her husband and a loving mother and grandmother. Now she has added to this influential ministry by becoming a writer. I have just finished reading her first book, titled *A Woman Adorned*, and predict this will also result in touching the hearts of many women who read it. I highly recommend this book!"

— Dr. H. L. Willmington;
Founder & Dean, Willmington School of the Bible
Founder & Dean, Liberty Home Bible Institute; Professor,
Rawlings School of Divinity @ Liberty University

"Wanda Wilson has taken the principles of the Bible and applied them over many years as an Evangelist's wife. She writes from a wealth of experience and heartfelt purpose in teaching women in very practical ways to stand strong in these days of great upheaval in our world. What makes this book so relevant is she has a life testimony of living out these truths in very difficult circumstances throughout her life. Wanda is full of energy and enthusiasm in expressing her desire to see other women walk in truth."

— Eva Middleton
Executive Assistant,
Willmington School of the Bible
Liberty University School of Divinity

"It was in 1976 when Wanda and I first met. The late Dr. Jerry Falwell and I were discussing the ministry of evangelism where I was serving at that time at Lakewood Campground in Myrtle Beach, SC. At his suggestion, I put together a team of young people from Liberty University to assist in the summer ministry established there. Wanda served for several years as part of that team, and we've maintained a close relationship for over 40 years now! By faith, she left her familiar surroundings, and we witnessed her eagerness to share her deep love for Jesus. My wife, Peggy, and I consider her and Johnny close friends! Though much has changed through the years, the one thing that remains constant is her love and faith in Jesus. She continues to minister with an insight for reaching others with the gospel through music, conferences and various areas of evangelism....And now through the writing of this book."

— **Jimmy Morse,**
Chaplain Emeritus, Lakewood Camping Resort Ministry;
President, Reach Out for Christ Ministries

"Wanda Wilson is a woman of God whom I've known personally for more than 10 years now. She has impacted my life and the many other women in El Salvador, especially during her time at Bethel Baptist Church in Apopa. Her work as an evangelist and teacher will leave a legacy in our hearts."

— **Cecy de Martinez,**
Pastor's Wife, Bethel Baptist Church,
Apopa, El Salvador

CONTENTS

PREFACE

In my early years of travel in this ministry with my husband, I would host ladies' teas as part of the crusades held in cooperation with a number of churches in the area. I've always loved writing, and it has been my bucket list dream to one day publish a book as an extension of this ministry to which the Lord has called us. I would lightly comment, "If I were to write a book, it would be entitled *It Happened When Johnny Was Out of Town.*" As a mother with small boys, I limited my travel so I could be at home with them. As soon as Johnny would leave town for the next meeting, an appliance would stop working, the guys would get sick, or the car would break down. Various other situations would also arise, but these are just a few. I knew the Lord was about to do His greatest work when the gospel was preached where Johnny was and my faith would be tested in his absence. Through this and many other life experiences, I learned that my sole dependence had to be on the Lord and Him alone — and I'm still learning!

First, I would like to thank the Lord for His undying faithfulness to me and this work that He has entrusted to my family. I have always believed this to be His calling, not only for Johnny in the work of evangelism but for me and our entire family as well. This special calling has given us the confidence that "Faithful is he that called you, who will also do it" (1 Thessalonians 5:24).

Second, thank you, Johnny, for allowing me to learn to depend on the Lord first and then entrusting me with every decision I had to make to remedy the situation that occurred once you left town. Now that takes faith!

Finally, I am thankful for the life of Mrs. Celeste Wemp, who is enjoying the glories of heaven now, for entrusting to me the wonderful opportunity to continue what she started many years ago when I sat under her during those ladies' events where she was the guest speaker and I went along as the singer. I watched the key women as they stood alongside their husbands, who had leadership positions in the church, to learn from them as a young girl seeking God's direction in my own life. There was no doubt in my mind even then that the Lord was preparing me for future ministry. It was my deepest heart's desire to marry the man who had been called by God to serve Him, and He has certainly met that desire! I am grateful beyond words for Chelsea, Sharon, Liz, and many others who have encouraged me along the way and have given me aid in the completion of this project. As well as my wonderful husband, thank you to all who have not let me rest until this book was written. You know who you are! You prayed, encouraged me, and believed in me when I felt pretty inadequate. May you all know how very much you have enriched my life! Thank you!

INTRODUCTION

Window-shopping—call it what you will, but you and I
know that more money has been spent on this one venture
alone than on the carefully prepared list one makes before
entering a store. Of this, I can speak with firsthand and
practiced knowledge. Advertisers know exactly what it
takes to lure the woman (and, yes, the man as well!) right
past the threshold of the store straight to the cash register.
I recall even as a young teenager, fresh out of high school,
what was expected of me when I got my first big job as
a window dresser at a ladies' dress shop in a local mall.
In my venture to collect, coordinate, and accessorize the
things needed for the mannequins at the front of the store,
I would also set aside items that would make their way
home with me.

And what woman doesn't envy and long to emulate
someone who has it together in her attire? From a young
age, many girls are intrigued with beauty pageants, top
celebrities, and planning their fantasy weddings—down
to the final details. I'm one of five girls. My sisters and
I were taught at a young age, respectfully, how to dress
appropriately as a young lady should—to the benefit of
my mom and dad. Even with tomboyish tendencies myself,

there was no walking out the front door without my parents' final approval of what I was wearing.

Well, my time in ladies' fashions was cut short by the Lord's intervention. He had other plans for me. My best friend from high school left for college right after graduation, and I was invited by her parents to visit her one weekend at what was then the Lynchburg Baptist College in Lynchburg, Virginia. It was during this visit that I answered the call of the Lord to do the same. I immediately sensed the hand of the Lord working in the life of my friend and longed to be where young people my own age were walking in the direction of God's leading. I also knew that if I were to marry a man called by God (which was my heart's desire), I had to be where they were as well.

I accepted Christ as my Savior at the young age of twelve, even though I was reared in church from the time I was in my mother's womb. My spiritual growth consisted of personal Bible reading, tithing, and even witnessing to my classmates in school, but the Lord made it clear to me that He was preparing me for a work that would only come about with added study of the Bible. I enrolled in the Thomas Road Bible Institute, which is now Willmington School of the Bible, where I spent two years under the teaching of Dr. Harold Willmington, Dr. and Mrs. Sumner Wemp, and many others to whom I owe much gratitude and credit for where I am today.

It was during a ladies' retreat that I heard Mrs. Wemp speak on "The Wise-Hearted Woman's Wardrobe," where she used Galatians 5:22–23. I was asked to go along to do the special music but was enthralled by the visual teaching of using an accessory to represent each of the fruit of the Spirit. They were added to a white dress, which symbolized the garment of salvation. You can only imagine how this captured my attention and interest.

Now, some thirty-plus years later, I'm doing the same with the very notes she entrusted to me just before the Lord called her home to heaven. The notes I had taken during the retreat were burned in a fire in our home in 1998. Although I could remember a lot of the material, I knew it lacked added scripture and other important points used by Celeste. Johnny, my husband, was on the phone one day with Dr. Wemp, and I asked to speak with Celeste after his conversation. When I shared with her all the events that had taken place since that first time she and I served together and how I longed to carry the baton and continue what she had started, she graciously agreed to send her original notes. How my heart was blessed! It was shortly thereafter that she passed away.

I have been entrusted to carry on this *visible expression of a spiritual reality* in these ladies' events I've been doing for over thirty years now. This teaching on Galatians 5:22–23 is very visual and appealing to women everywhere. I've heard studies confirm that 65 percent of the population learns more through methods of visual teaching.

What woman doesn't like a wedding? There are not too many things more beautiful than a bride in her wedding gown. Christ refers to the redeemed as "the bride of Christ." The picture that has repeatedly come to mind is what a bride does to prepare herself for the day when she stands before the altar to commit herself to the one who will be her husband. She meticulously chooses the gown and every accessory to adorn that gown with grave anticipation—mindful of every detail. With this in mind, I've changed the title to *A Woman Adorned*.

As I begin this teaching regarding the fruit of the Spirit, I'm wearing a white dress that signifies salvation. I have chosen a gold belt to represent love, applied gold jewelry to represent joy (gold, a rare and valuable metal, denotes purity), and put on red shoes (with red signifying the blood of Christ) to represent peace. I chose a red jacket for long-suffering and wear white gloves to represent gentleness (think of the phrase, "to handle with kid gloves"). For goodness, I chose a white purse because giving is an outflow of generosity from one who has been shown generosity. A gold watch represents faith, as we keep in mind the faithfulness of a life dedicated to serving the Lord. I wear a red hat, which in earlier years was a symbol of submission, for meekness. And finally, I use hair spray to represent temperance (giving mention to a girdle as well) as we look at a life that is eager to display self-control—thus mastering our impulses.

Before stepping out the door, we take one last look in the mirror to make sure we approve of our outfit. What better mirror do we have as children of God than the Bible? God's Word is our mirror. It shows us the Father, who has been revealed to us through the sacrifice of His Son, Jesus.

The book concludes with instructions from the Word on how to walk in the Spirit every day. This is, of course, a woman adorned on the outside, but it is used to drive home the truth of how the ultimate change comes from within. As I mention quite repetitively throughout the book, the change takes place as we yield our lives to walk in obedience to the Lord through the power of the indwelling Holy Spirit. Every day, I realize the companionship I have with Christ because of His continual presence. Everything a child of God tries to do on his or her own ends in utter failure, but for those who rely on His Spirit, a glorious production of fruit appears—and it reaps eternal benefits!

The scripture teaches us so much about this wonderful person of the Holy Spirit and all He longs to do through each believer. First and foremost, He is *holy*. "But as he which hath called you is holy, so be ye holy in all manner of conversation; because it is written, Be ye holy; for I am holy" (1 Peter 1:15–16). By this alone, we understand that our calling, before and above everything else, is to holiness. My prayer is that we, as sisters in Christ, will set our hearts to this one thing. It takes our entire lifetime to understand all that this means and the mighty influence for the cause of Christ it exerts! As I mention in the final chapter on walking in the Spirit, we become fully aware of the battle that ensues between the Spirit and the flesh, but let me boldly remind you (and myself) that the battle has already been fought and won at Calvary. The Holy Spirit now works for the holiness in His people.

Holiness is a word of unfathomable meaning and reveals to us, His children, the purpose for which we were created. As angels were created to declare and proclaim God's glory, so we can bring Him glory through a life that is being conformed into His image. His highest glory, though, is given when the Holy Spirit uses us to then lead someone else into the saving knowledge of Christ. What a privilege of ours this is!

When I begin this teaching in the audience of other women, I carry a black dress. This symbolizes the condition of my life before coming to know Christ as my Savior. It is best described in Galatians 5:19–21 as the works of the flesh. For believers in Christ, by faith, "all things have become new" (2 Corinthians 5:17). What is it like to be new in Christ? The answer is that we are clothed differently. The old person has died with Christ, and the new one has been resurrected with Him. By the power of His Spirit, we don't talk the way we used to talk, we don't go to some places we used to go to, and we set our minds on things that bring God the glory. "If ye then be risen with Christ, seek those things which are above, where Christ sitteth on the right hand of God. Set your affections on things above, not on things of the earth. For ye are dead, and your life is hid with Christ in God" (Colossians 3:1–3). It's a choice!

We choose God's holiness, and by faith, we walk in His holiness. It involves a constant surrendering to the Holy Spirit as we walk hand in hand in step with Him. And as we study this together, allow me to encourage you to grow in that walk. Learning the truths of God's Word is fun! As you allow the Holy Spirit to produce His fruit in your life, may He use you mightily for His glory!

Several Bible translations are used in my studies, but I chose the King James Version for the scriptures given. Most of my memorization from childhood came from this version, and to this day, I love the poetic flow it affords. The basic outline used by Mrs. Wemp is the same. My desire is to dedicate this not only to my daughters-in-law and the granddaughters who are becoming a growing part of our family but to each woman I have the privilege of meeting in this wonderful ministry with which I have been entrusted.

With humbleness of heart, accompanied by overwhelming thanksgiving, I see that the Lord continues to use this study in places all over the United States and El Salvador (and beyond) to this very day! I'm thankful too for the many men and women the Lord has placed in my path to encourage and help me grow in my walk with the Lord. It is my prayer that as you read this book, you will be blessed with understanding the work of the Holy Spirit in His application of the fruit of the Spirit in your life and realize "Strength and honor are her clothing, and she shall rejoice in time to come" (Proverbs 3:25).

CHAPTER 1

The Garment of Salvation

(The White Dress)

Behold, God is my salvation; I will trust and not be afraid: for the Lord Jehovah is my strength and my song; he also is become my salvation.

—Isaiah 12:2

I shall greatly rejoice in the Lord, my soul shall be joyful in my God: for He hath clothed me with the garments of salvation, He hath covered me with the robe of righteousness, as a bridegroom decks himself with ornaments, and as a bride adorns herself with her jewels.

—Isaiah 61:10

Oh, if we could just sit down together over a good cup of coffee and hear every testimony and share all the details of how every person came to Christ as Savior! To this day, this is something I enjoy when I'm traveling or meeting someone for the first time. My story of being brought up in the church as a little girl and coming to know Christ at the young age of twelve is not the same as my husband's. He was able to witness his own mother's salvation experience, though he didn't fully understand all that was taking place as a young guy. It was a high school teacher, a faithful layman in his church, who visited him one day (while he was engrossed in a baseball game on the television) and invited him to vacation Bible school (VBS). When Mr. Little invited him and his brothers to come, he also asked, "What are the three great days on the Christian calendar?"

Not to be written off as a twelve-year-old who knew nothing of the things of the church, Johnny answered, "Christmas, the day Jesus left heaven and was born; Easter, the day Jesus died and rose from the dead and returned to heaven; and homecoming." He answered this way because these were basically the days he remembered attending church. He tells the story that some sort of food was served on these days, and that was what he remembered (and enjoyed!) the most. The whole idea of going to church on a regular basis did not even exist for him until his mother's conversion.

His father was a truck driver who transported new vehicles to various car dealerships in many states. This meant he was on the road all the time. When he was home (which was usually on Sunday), this was the only time he spent on the farm and with the family, so attending church wasn't even given a thought. Well, Mr. Little was quite taken aback by this young man's response and added, "We are going to learn about the second coming of Christ during this time in VBS and would love for you and your brothers and friends to come as well." It's funny to hear Johnny tell the story as he preaches because he shares that his immediate response to Christ coming back again was, "Really? Is He coming this Sunday? If He is, I'll be there!" It was said with instant, childlike honesty, but I chuckle every time I hear him tell it. Johnny goes on to share that after the first day of VBS, he was pretty disturbed over all Mr. Little had shared concerning Christ's return. He couldn't explain it but goes on to say that the next day, after everyone finished singing and just before he took off on his bike to head back home, Mr. Little approached him yet again and said, "Wow, that was some good singing, huh? You know, we all will be singing together one day in heaven. Will you be there?"

Without a moment's hesitation, Johnny admitted that he wouldn't be there because he had never asked Jesus into his heart. It was then that Mr. Little took Johnny through the scriptures and shared with him God's plan of salvation and Johnny prayed and asked the Lord to save him.

You see, that's what salvation means. It has a twofold implication that people are lost, sick, or in need, thereby needing someone to find them or rescue them from their present state. It all started with the fall of man in the Garden of Eden. The wonderful news is that even before the foundation of the world, the Father had us on His mind and provided the way of salvation through His Son, Jesus. He is the source of salvation! We can begin with Genesis 3 and continue throughout the rest of the Bible to Revelation to see how God made a way of salvation for all people and "…is longsuffering to us-ward, not willing that any should perish but that all should come to repentance" (2 Peter 3:9).

When I was growing up, going to church when the doors were open was something as natural for me as attending school on the opening day. I was taught the stories from the Bible, sang hymns from the hymnal, and memorized scripture right along with everyone else. The eye-opener came one particular evening though when I was attending a special youth rally and saw a movie that showed the reality of heaven and hell as described in the Bible. At the conclusion, the youth leader asked for a show of hands of all who had personally asked for forgiveness of their sins and surrendered themselves to Christ. He mentioned what Christ had done to redeem all His creation so that no one would be cursed to eternal damnation in this horrible place called hell. He reemphasized what was stated in the film—that hell was created for the devil and his angels, it was God's intention that all people have the personal choice of heaven, and this was exactly why Christ died, was buried, and rose again. He made it clear that it was not possible to go to heaven on the merits of my father or mother or especially by any good that I had done. Salvation is personal and is accompanied with a personal step of repentance and faith. I couldn't raise my hand! It was right at this moment I knew that the Lord was speaking to me.

When the plea was made for those who wanted to make the decision to give their heart and life to the Lord, I was one of the first to make my way to the altar. The Bible stories and verses I had learned and memorized had new meaning. I sang the hymns with a new-found joy and a longing to praise the one who gave His life for me! I also realized that it was now up to me to share this good news of God's love with someone else.

When we look at who we are apart from Christ, it's not a pretty picture but a very vivid one.

> Now the works of the flesh are manifest, which are these: adultery, fornication, uncleanness, lasciviousness, idolatry, witchcraft, hatred, variance, emulations, wrath, strife, seditions, heresies, envyings, murders, drunkenness, revellings, and such like, of the which I tell you before, as I have also told you in time past, that

they which do such things shall not inherit the
kingdom of God. (Galatians 5:21)

To say the least, we are black with sin and deserving of
eternal separation from God! All kinds of ugliness is still
wrapped up in each one of those acts of rebellion, but just
in case anything at all was left out, notice the "and such
like" at the end of our self-portrait. It's been said before,
but let me emphasize again, that the Spirit who indwells
the believer is first and foremost *holy* in His nature and
works for the holiness of His people. Not only is Jesus the
way to perfect communion with the Father in providing
salvation, but it is also in Him we "…move, and live, and
breathe, and have our being" (Acts 17:28).

In this work of evangelism, I've witnessed individuals
coming to the saving knowledge of Christ in various ways
and from various backgrounds. Whether I am in a one-
on-one or a classroom or crusade setting, my desire is
to be used by the Lord as I depend on His power and
wisdom to simply be obedient. In area-wide events we join
efforts with members from local churches who volunteer
to be counselors for those who want to come forward for
salvation during the service. We offer training during
the weeks leading up to the event to encourage and help
those who sign up. Pastors are nearby to aid in any and all
questions that may arise beyond the process of leading an
individual to Christ.

I recall one particular situation in a local meeting
where a lady from the church was diligently helping a
woman who was under conviction and made her way
forward. She was crying and made it very clear that she
needed salvation, but she began telling the counselor about
how she was presently living with a man to whom she was
not married. She was unloading a lot of distressing details
and had questions as to how things would unfold once she

returned back to her everyday life. The counselor saw that this was a situation where she needed the intervention of the pastor. After the pastor was given the information, he then proceeded to get Johnny to gain advice as to how to handle it appropriately. Once Johnny started speaking with her, he immediately knew that it was best that I should talk with her myself.

With grave emotion, this lady expressed one more time her concerns about the lifestyle she was living; she knew in her heart that changes had to be made. In reality, she wanted me to specifically tell her step-by-step what to do. My first questions to her were, "Did you come forward for salvation? Do you know the Lord as your Savior?" She indicated emphatically that that was why she was there. My response to her at this point was, "Well then, let's take care of that first! May I help you in this prayer of salvation? I believe that once we take care of this need in your life, the Lord will direct you in knowing how to handle all the rest. Can we do that?"

"Oh, yes!" she said.

As we bowed our heads together in prayer, I witnessed this dear lady giving her heart to Christ. Once the prayer was over, she gripped my hand and said, "I believe I know what to do now! Just now, while we were praying, it was as if it became so clear to me!" Without asking for any more details, I offered to pray for wisdom for her in her walk with Christ and encouraged her to find a local church that would help her grow in her relationship with the Lord.

We are citizens of a world foreign to the nature of God. Since the fall of man after creation, we move to the impulses of the decision to go our own way. However, once God invades our world and opens our eyes to the depravity of sin, He offers us a new life and lifestyle. The woman, Jackie (this is not her real name, but for the sake of respect and anonymity, this is what I'll call her), is just one example of this.

I was involved in a summer ministry with a music team where we did concerts, conducted youth and adult activities, and did one-on-one evangelism with the purpose of sharing the Good News of Christ on a daily basis. This was where I met Jackie. The chaplain who headed the ministry was conducting devotions one morning when a knock came on the door where we gathered. In a voice that could barely be heard, a young lady on the other side of the door asked for me. She introduced herself and began sharing how she had heard my testimony the night before during a music concert.

As I led her away to a private place to talk, she began sharing details of a life of alcohol and drugs. What gnawed at her more than all that was the fact that she had had an abortion at an early age. The guilt of it all was weighing on her heavily. "Could God forgive me for something like this?" she asked.

Before I answered her question, I had to admit that I knew nothing of the lifestyle she had described. What I did share though was the fact that this was why Christ died. There was no difference between her sin and my sin, but Christ gave His life so we would be free from the guilt and destruction it brought about. I shared with her God's plan of salvation and asked if she would like to give her heart to Christ. She didn't make the decision right then, but we formed a friendship and I continued to express to her a personal need for Christ. Eventually, she gave her heart and life to Christ, and I even had the opportunity to witness to her parents as well!

The white garment of salvation that we possess was purchased by the precious blood of Jesus, and the only stains it should bear are the stains of the blood He shed for us. We can say with glad "Hallelujahs" today and throughout eternity that *He* has covered us with the robe of righteousness, and though our sins be as scarlet, they shall be white as snow. "These are they who have come out of the great tribulation and washed their robes and made them white in the blood of the Lamb" (Revelation 7:14). Our salvation is complete! Now it is essential that we "Adorn the doctrine of God our Savior in all things. For the grace of God that brings salvation hath appeared to all men" (Titus 2:10b–11).

How did you come to the saving knowledge of Christ? I would love to hear every detail. You now wear the white dress, which is the robe of righteousness. Now, stay with me as we learn together how to adorn that white dress through the power of the Holy Spirit!

Prayer
Father in heaven, I believe what Your Word says is true in proclaiming every person a sinner, myself included. Thank You for giving Your Son Jesus to be the perfect sacrifice for my sin. I come to You by faith, asking for forgiveness, accepting Christ as my Savior and Lord of my life, starting right now. Thank You for dying for me. Help me, Lord, by the power of Your Holy Spirit to live for You. In the Name of Jesus I pray. Amen.

CHAPTER 2

Love

(The Gold Belt)

Love not the world, neither the things that are in the world. If any man love the world, the love of the Father is not in him.

—1 John 2:15

Hereby perceive we the love of God, because he laid down his life for us: and we ought to lay down our lives for the brethren. But whoso hath this world's good, and seeth his brother have need, and shutteth up his bowels of compassion from him, how dwelleth the love of God in him?

—1 John 3:16–17

Just as the belt embraces the whole garment, so love embraces all the fruit. I chose gold to signify God's pure *agapao* (agape) love. We now add a gold belt to the white dress of salvation because it represents a metal that is considered to be very rare, even compared to diamonds. *Gold* is derived from the Old English word meaning "yellow." It is one of the heaviest metals in the world, yet it is so soft that it can be molded with the hands. Very few chemicals can attack gold; that's why it keeps its shine, even when buried for thousands of years. According to some, there's enough gold on the earth's crust to cover the entire land surface knee-deep.

There are also 182 scriptures found in the Bible that speak of gold. It refers to lips of knowledge being more precious than gold in Proverbs 20:15, which says, "There is gold, and a multitude of rubies: but the lips of knowledge are a precious jewel." Think on that one for a while. Many relationships where love once blossomed have been destroyed over a single word spoken in the heat of anger. Although our minds cannot fully comprehend its grandeur, Revelation 21 describes the "city of our God" (heaven) as being a "city of gold" where we, God's people, will one day dwell throughout eternity. Even our faith, in the eyes of the Lord, is described in terms of gold. "That the trial of your faith, being much more precious than of gold that perisheth, though it be tried with fire, might be found unto praise and honour and glory at the appearing of Jesus Christ" (1 Peter 1:7). Let me encourage you today, Sisters in Christ; all you may be going through right now in your walk with the Lord as you depend on Him has great value. Press on!

There was the censer, the Ark of the Covenant, the pot that contained the manna from heaven, Aaron's rod, and the tablets of the covenant, which were covered in gold, all located in the Holy of Holies within the tabernacle. Our love for Christ is a faith-based display of how we obey Him. Psalm 19 describes God's Word to be His law, His testimony, His statute, His commandment, and His judgment (Psalm 19:9). This is all very enlightening, but

Psalm 19:10 says, "More to be desired are they than gold, yea, than much fine gold; sweeter also than honey and the honeycomb." Do we treasure God's greatest love story to humanity just that way?

As we begin studying the fruit of the Spirit, we must take time to wrap our thoughts around the dominating fact that the author of Galatians is not speaking of various fruits but of a single fruit—the fruit of the Spirit. Love, joy, peace, long-suffering, gentleness, goodness, faith, meekness, and temperance are but phrases and descriptions of one fruit, which is love itself. Joy can be described as love taking flight like a bird that has been pushed from the nest, realizing the limitless capacity to view more than just the area to which it was formerly confined. Peace is love reserving a moment of flight to take refuge and finding the safe haven under God's wings. "He who dwelleth in the secret place of the most High, shall abide under the shadow of the Almighty" (Psalm 91:1). Long-suffering is basking in the assurance of enduring love with an unwavering confidence that there is a High Priest who has suffered as well and is compassionate in His thoughts toward His creation. Gentleness broadens the scope of the child of God and is love on the social level. Goodness is love in action, as we see others the way God sees us. Faith is a confiding love that persuades us that He who began His work in us will also complete it unto the day of Jesus Christ (Philippians 1:6). Meekness is love, washing another's feet with a willingness to show humility in putting someone else before our own self-interests. Finally, temperance is genuine self-love with a proper balance of personal interests so as to exercise Jesus's command to love our neighbor as ourselves (Mark 12:31).

If you were to randomly ask every other person you meet on the street the meaning of love, most would describe it as an emotion or uncontrollable passion. There are emotions that exist as a result of love, but it's not so much an emotion as a choice. Human love has its own limitations. The love of a mother toward her children, the love of a patriot who willingly gives his or her life for his or her country, the affectionate love of husband and wife, and the philanthropist who gives to whom he or she chooses are affections that we should never ignore or disregard. The annals of history tell us much in the realm of the effectual display in all of these. We choose to conduct ourselves toward another person in a way that we, personally, would want to be treated ourselves. It's a commitment. Jesus commanded us to love Him first and then love our neighbor as ourselves. We learn from Him that love is a quality that is not natural but is given to us through His Spirit as a gift of divine grace. It's pretty difficult to command an emotion!

Laws are made when the flesh produces the things listed in Galatians 5:19–21, but when we talk about the fruit of the Spirit, Galatians 5:23(b) says, "against such there is no law," because the fruit comes from God. The day we give our heart to Christ, we begin a life of obedience and devotion to the one who loved us from the very start! Love is a gift and not a natural quality, whose very root is *charis*, or grace. Our entire Christian walk—loving the unlovely, the stranger, and those unworthy—is the love of God imparted to us through the Holy Spirit, who resides within us. No effort of our will or work will produce love; it comes down to us and is shed abroad in our hearts by the Spirit. Oh, what a gift of grace! And since it is a gift, it involves no merit whatsoever on the part of the one receiving it. To Jesus Christ be all the glory!

There are basically three kinds of love. The first Greek word for love is *eros* (the stem of the word *erotic*), which is currently displayed through media to depict exploits in the realm of the physical—it satisfies the flesh. People fall in and out of this kind of love every day, but it's also reserved for the physical love between a man and a woman who have been joined together in marriage. It is an erotic love that is depicted in the story of King David in 2 Samuel 11, when he looked from his window one evening (while his own men were on the battlefield) to see Bathsheba bathing on her rooftop. He then lusted after her, ordered her to his chambers, and then committed adultery—even with the knowledge of her being married. Before we are too harsh on this one, who was also called "a man after God's own heart," I need to especially remind myself, "Therefore let him who thinks he stands take heed lest he fall" (1 Corinthians 10:12). God's Word also reminds us, "Do not commit adultery, but I say to you that everyone who looks at a woman in order to covet her has already committed adultery with her in his heart" (Matthew 5:27–28). Ladies, there's no need to think of this as being a warning directed to only men. Our prayer should be that God will teach us to keep our eyes, hearts, and minds clean before Him. We need to remember, "For all that is in the world, the lust of the flesh, and the lust of the eyes, and the pride of life, is not of the Father, but is of the world" (1 John 2:16).

The second *phileo*, which means "brotherly love" (as in Philadelphia, the City of Brotherly Love), is demonstrated through friendship. One good example of this is the friendship between David and Jonathan in the Old Testament. There's nothing like having that special friend with whom, no matter the time or distance, you're able to pick right back up where you left off in a previous encounter. I'm thankful for friends like that!

Lastly, *agapao* (agape) is the divine love, God's unmerited love, which is offered to all humankind, who were made in the image of God. This means that He loves us just the way we are! Too many times, we try to be someone we're not when it comes to gaining a relationship with another person. It's hard to comprehend being loved when we feel unlovable.

When I speak of God's agape love, 1 Corintians 13 comes to mind right away. The description of love given here lists qualities that tell another person whether or not we bear the fruit of the Spirit in the area of love. Here's the list.

- Love suffers long—meaning you are patient with those who beforehand had a tendency to rub you the wrong way.
- Love doesn't envy what someone else has.
- Love is not boastful—one does not elevate oneself above someone else.
- Love is not easily provoked—you don't fly off the handle at the least little offense.
- Love rejoices in the truth—whereas before you took delight in engaging in bad gossip about someone else, now you want to see the good, ending the gossip!
- Love bears, believes, and hopes when others give up. All of these have exceeded the realm of emotion, right? They're also actions that we are far from capable of apart from Christ.

I was encouraged by a longtime friend of the ministry when Johnny and I had the opportunity to meet with him during one of our trips to Oklahoma. He was now up in years but still served faithfully in the work of evangelism until his wife became ill and was confined to a wheelchair. He has lovingly and faithfully cared for her for a long time. This, my friend, is a commitment to love and a great example to us all of a union bound by marital vows. There are many stories that could be told of those in prestigious positions who have stepped down and even left a job for the sole purpose of caring for someone they loved. We've witnessed spouses doing the same when one or the other was diagnosed with Alzheimer's or other crippling diseases. Sometimes couples are separated and divorced as a result of these circumstances.

I remember as a little girl, before giving my heart to Christ, memorizing John 3:16. As a growing Christian, who is supposed to be constantly changed into Christ's image as I spend time with Him day by day, I also realize that people who cross my path in my down-to-earth connections should see His love in me as well. What I say, where I go, how I react or respond to everyday circumstances tell a far greater story. Colossians 3:14 says, "And above all these things put on charity (love), which is the bond of perfectness."

This brought to mind a sermon I heard by the late Adrian Rogers, for whose ministry I prayed so many years. It was entitled "Christlike Love," and he began with the story from John 13 of the example of Jesus's love in washing the disciples' feet. He began with a statement from a psychiatrist, who said, "The greatest need mankind has is to love and to be loved." In a world where iniquity abounds, love waxes cold, thereby making the need for exhibiting God's love a grave responsibility for the people of God. Dr. Rogers continued on with four major points:

1. Christlike love is selfless love. Jesus laid aside His garments for the sole purpose of washing His disciples' feet.
2. Christlike love is steadfast love. John 13:1 says, "...He loved them unto the end." The lovely and the unlovely He loves because of His great grace.
3. Christlike love is serving love. First John 3:18 says, "My little children, let us not love in word, neither in tongue, but in deed and in truth." Love

is not giving people what they deserve, but what they need.

4. Christlike love is sanctifying love. I'm so glad that I didn't have to fit into the "perfect" category to receive God's divine love, aren't you?

"By this shall all men know that you are my disciples, if you have love one for another" (John 13:35). Love is more than just playing a role. One of the main discouragements I faced as a young believer was the difference I witnessed in the way people behaved when they attended church and taught Sunday School and the way they conducted themselves outside of church. They didn't always match up. As I mature in the Word and my walk with Christ, He is daily pointing out the areas that need to be honed in my own life. When I'm in a situation where someone's personality is far different from my own, it can create challenges and differences of opinions that could result in negative confrontations if I'm not relying solely on the Holy Spirit for discernment. He allows me to "disagree agreeably" and create in another way an opportunity to make friends with someone who could potentially be an enemy. "And hope maketh not ashamed; because the love of God is shed abroad in our hearts by the Holy Ghost which is given unto us" (Romans 5:5).

When Jesus was teaching His disciples what are called "the Beatitudes" during His Sermon on the Mount in Matthew 5, He ended with the topic of loving our neighbor and our enemy. He was also asked one time during His short ministry on earth, "Who is our neighbor?" He made it very clear that our neighbor also included our enemy, else we were no better than the heathen. I like what John Stott said from *Through the Bible, Through the Year*:

If we love only those who love us, we are no better than unbelievers. If we love our enemies, however, it will be apparent that we are children of our heavenly Father, since His love is indiscriminate, giving rain and sunshine to all people alike. Alfred Plummer summed up the options: "To return evil for good is devilish. To return good for good is human. To return good for evil is divine." (pg. 195)

Matthew 5:45 says, "That ye may be the children of your Father which is in heaven; for he maketh the sun to rise on the evil and on the good; and sendeth rain on the just and on the unjust." Although so much more could be said regarding this fruit of the Spirit called love, I want to leave you with this. With the power of the indwelling Holy Spirit, we can love the Savior, the saints, and the sinners — enemies included!

Prayer

Father, thank You for loving me even before I confessed You as Savior. My heart's desire is that the Holy Spirit would love through me so that all may know that I serve a great and mighty God. In the Name of Jesus I pray. Amen.

CHAPTER 3

(The Gold Jewelry)

My brethren, count it all joy when ye fall into divers temptations; Knowing this, that the trying of your faith worketh patience. But let patience have her perfect work, that ye may be perfect and entire, wanting nothing.

—James 1:2–4

Joy, the second of the fruit of the Spirit, is represented with gold jewelry. Again, gold depicts the purest of all metals, and jewelry is attractive and complements the outfit. Very rarely do you see a woman walk out of her house without some sort of accessory in the form of jewelry. Even if she were to put on a dress that she has owned for a very long time, all it takes is a different necklace, earrings, or a bracelet to spruce it up to where it looks brand new. I am a woman, so trust me on this! There are times when funds are low, and a new dress or an addition to the wardrobe is just not an option.

I remember vividly in high school when I had the option to elect a home economics course. The topic turned from things of the home to expanding one's wardrobe by mixing and matching items and accessories. This all resulted in a new outfit without having to purchase anything more than an inexpensive scarf or other item to change things up. To this day, I still do just that. I've found this to be an area that interested me so much that I ended up in ladies' fashions right after graduation as an assistant manager. The job came about as I was being observed while dressing a display window in a woman's clothing store. My hours were slim and the pay almost the same! I guess it brings a heart full of gratitude for being one of five girls and learning frugality. I watched my mom use great ingenuity in everything from food to furniture to fashion. She taught us all to make the best of what we had.

In the area of "joy," though, we have the mighty Holy Spirit within who is the very source of the believer's joy. This fruit is truly a complimentary gift that when exercised can be detected right away. Proverbs 15:13 and 15 has this to say: "A merry heart makes a cheerful countenance; but by sorrow of the heart the spirit is broken....All the days of the afflicted are evil; but he that is of a merry heart has a continual feast."

One of my favorite lessons as a youth in my local church programs was when I solidified the truths of joy by breaking it down into an acrostic: J—Jesus, O—others, and Y—you. This is a simple, yet very profound lesson. Jesus is to have preeminence in the life of the believer. "Seek ye first the kingdom of God and His righteousness, and all these things shall be added unto you" (Matthew 6:33). A life of faith means that I can have full confidence that the Lord knows what is needed in my life from food and clothing to all things beyond! He supplies and longs for me to put Him first. I am to esteem others more highly than I do myself by treating them as I would be treated. Finally, I am to die to self daily and take up my cross and follow Jesus. A broken and contrite heart before the Lord helps me to accomplish His will and discover real joy in the process!

I'll never forget the years that my two oldest sons were serving in the military after the tragic fall of the Twin Towers in New York in September 2001. There was a sense of fear and uncertainty that prevailed. You can only imagine the emotions arising in me as the news came in on a regular basis, telling of those who had lost their lives in both Iraq and Afghanistan. I had a son in each of those places! Whether I was in church or talking randomly with someone I had met at work or in the streets, the conversation would center around our military men and women. Those who knew our boys always asked about them and requested that I relay to them their appreciation for what they were doing. Many would ask, "How are you able to function? You seem to be so calm and at peace about where they are right now!"

My response would always be, "The same God that I trusted for their protection when they got on the school bus on the first day of school is the same God I trust for their protection now! I can joyfully say that they gave their hearts to Christ in our home at an early age. If they lose their lives while protecting our country, my heart will ache as it has never ached before, but I know I'll see them again! My joy comes from this assurance!" This was an opportunity not only to witness to those who didn't know the Lord but also to encourage those who knew the Lord and longed for joy in a situation where joy could not be found.

"It is a great thing to count it all joy. Counting is not the language of poetry or sentiment, but of cold, unerring calculation. It adds up the column thus: sorrow, temptation, difficulty, opposition, depression, desertion, danger, discouragement on every side, but at the bottom of the column is God's presence, God's will, God's joy, God's promise, God's recompense" (A. B. Simpson, chapter 9—"*The Spirit of Comfort*").

Anyone who knows me also knows that I have thoroughly enjoyed *My Utmost for His Highest* by Oswald Chambers. Here's what he has to say regarding joy: "Joy comes from seeing the complete fulfillment of the specific purpose for which I was created and born again; not from successfully doing something of my own choosing, but doing what the Father chose for me to do, just as Jesus did" (devotional for March 5, "*Is He Really Lord?*").

Joy is more intense than happiness. It lasts far beyond the things that tend to make us happy. "These things I write unto you that your joy may be full" (1 John 1:4). John was one of Jesus's twelve apostles. He was writing to a group of believers to encourage them in their service for the Lord. Perhaps they had lost a zeal that was once evident in serving the Lord. John had personally witnessed Christ's wisdom, love, and miracles. He saw His death, burial, and the miracle of His resurrection. Now it was up to John to declare to these believers what was theirs in full power because of the resurrection. They could have full access to the Father too! Christ's act was not just for a chosen few, and the Holy Spirit would allow them to have an all-sufficient communion with each other and share in the benefits of a fullness of joy not found in possessions from this world. John was their cheerleader! He saw in this group of believers the potential to know joy and to be the ones used by God to pass it on to others.

Batman and Superman were household names when my three guys were growing up. I have to chuckle every time I think about moving the furniture in my sons' bedroom when we moved from one house to another; I discovered a Batman symbol that had been discreetly drawn on the wall. It was in the closet too, only to be found once all the clothes were removed. I thought the existence of these imaginary figures would be a short-lived phase — not so. Those superheroes are as popular today as they were then! Who doesn't love a hero? The situation might be dim, and it might appear as though evil will win over what everyone thinks is good and right — until the hero comes! With clever skill, strength, and power, the hero is the one to save the day when defeat looks imminent. This is exactly what we have in Christ. He is our hero! He defeated Satan, the god of this world, and reigns victorious over sin and death. "The joy of the Lord is your strength" (Nehemiah 8:10b).

In my recent study of *Esther* by Beth Moore, she challenged my thoughts regarding both of these emotions we experience in a lifetime, and I'd like to share a quote of hers from this study to explain a bit further. It began with verse twelve from Psalm 139, which says, "Yea, the darkness hideth not from Thee; but the night shineth as the day; the darkness and the light are both alike to Thee." God used Esther "at such a time as this" (Esther 4:14) as an instrument in the deliverance of the Jews; Esther, chapter 8, verse 17, describes to us, the reader, the gladness and rejoicing that permeated the city after a period of mourning and darkness. Beth goes on to say that happiness means "lightness." Indeed, you and I could probably tell story after story of those days of darkness and the overwhelming release that came when the Lord intervened and brought lightness and rejoicing once again. Yes, circumstances change, and for that we can be very thankful, but it also takes the grace of God for us to experience His joy during the dark times. I appreciate this statement from Beth:

The day never seems brighter than when we walk out of a pitch-black room, does it? Beloved, when a moment like this comes, we need to take it. We often speak of happiness as a less noble term than joyfulness because the former is circumstantial and the latter less conditional; but when God intervenes in our circumstances and we get a chance not only to know we've been blessed but feel blessed, nothing is more appropriate than seizing the happy moment. A time of happiness can come like a shot of B-12 to the soul to boost your system when darkness spreads once again like a virus. One of the hardest challenges about taking advantage of a God-given time of happiness is the guilt of knowing that it coincides with someone else's darkness. No, we don't flaunt our light in someone else's darkness, but surely we can find a way to dip ourselves in the bubble bath of a second's bliss when it comes. Even if all we do is lean our heads back in the sunshine of our soul's Sabbath and take a minute to feel the glad emotion; it is meant by God to be the medicine for our weary souls. Times of happiness are glimpses of heaven until we get there. Homesickness doesn't always feel sick. Sometimes it's a quick flash of happy that makes us long to find it and keep it.

To this, I say that happiness is the springboard that catapults us to new heights of joy and we ought not rule it out. Instead, we should realize that the God who designed us also longs for us to know and experience His joy. It's not something we can conjure up on our own! As a matter of fact, His Word tells us in John 1:10–12, "He was in the world and the world knew Him not. He came unto His own and His own received Him not. But, as many as received Him, to them gave He the power to become the sons of God, even to them that believe on His Name."

In the fourth book of James, there are questions hurled at believers regarding the origin of wars, fighting, rumors of war, envying, lusting, and all the things that come as a result of loving this world and the things in it or just simply the very presence of sin we now experience until we see Christ. The conclusion and remedy is also given in James 4:9–10, which says, "Be afflicted, and mourn, and weep; let your laughter be turned to mourning, and your joy to heaviness. Humble yourselves in the sight of the Lord, and He shall lift you up."

What has the Lord called you to do? Do you find real joy in knowing that you are right where you are supposed to be? Are you still seeking His face on this and trusting Him to bring lightness to a heart that may be experiencing darkness and heaviness right now? Jesus said in 1John 1:4, "These things I write unto you that your joy may be full." (That's my prayer for you as well!) Having the joy of the Lord as our strength literally means that we are delighting in Jehovah as our strong refuge. Allowing the Spirit to be our joy in a time of loss, turmoil, or encompassing confusion is an act of worship. Let the joy of the Lord be your strength today. It's an act of faith!

Prayer

Father, thank You for the Holy Spirit, who is my joy when darkness surrounds me! Forgive me for seeking for joy in the things of this world, and teach me to seek after righteousness and Your truth. May others look at me and see Your joy radiating from me as I trust You in all my circumstances. In the Name of Jesus I humbly pray. Amen.

CHAPTER 4

Peace

(The Red Shoes)

How beautiful on the mountains are the feet of those who bring good news, who proclaim peace, who proclaim righteousness, who say to Zion, your God reigns.

— Isaiah 52:7

Stand therefore, having your loins girt about with truth, and having on the breastplate of righteousness. And your feet shod with the preparation of the gospel of peace.

— Ephesians 6:14–15

I chose shoes to represent this third fruit of the Spirit — and they are red to remind us of the blood of Christ, which was shed for us so that we may know peace. As Isaiah prophesied the release of Israel from Babylonian captivity, he also prophesied of a greater deliverance of humankind through the person of Jesus Christ. Peace is a resolution of conflict. There was a presence of sin that came about with the disobedience of humankind in the Garden of Eden. We were given a choice, and we made the wrong choice. Jesus and Paul both spoke of this topic early in their ministries. Paul, in Romans 10:15, said, "And how shall they preach except they be sent? As it is written, how beautiful are the feet of them that preach the gospel of peace, and bring glad tidings of good things." Jesus also touches on Isaiah's prophesy in His first sermon, recorded in Luke 4:18–19, which says, "The Spirit of the Lord is upon me to preach the gospel to the poor; He hath sent me to heal the brokenhearted, to preach deliverance to the captives, and recovering of sight to the blind, to set at liberty them that are bruised, to preach the acceptable year of the Lord."

The irony in speaking peace is that it is not always accepted by everyone who hears it, as was the case in Jesus's first sermon. Let me remind you too that Christ Himself said, "Think not that I am come to send peace on earth; I came not to send peace, but a sword" (Matthew 10:34). It was just prior to this statement that He met with the disciples to send them out to preach, heal the sick, raise the dead, and cast out devils. Sickness, death, and a countless list of other maladies can bring unrest to a soul. This, in fact, is the opposite of peace. I've heard many a preacher say that the preaching of the gospel awakens an intense resentment—simply because it reveals to us just how unholy we are. Like a sword that pierces the soul, it then creates an intense yearning from within to do something about it. We can choose to die in our sin or by faith put our trust in the Prince of Peace. Jesus went on to remind them that it was the Spirit who would do the speaking and that even in imminent persecution, they were not to fear, but "preach it upon the housetops" (Matthew 10:27).

There are two kinds of peace: the peace *with* God and the peace *of* God. "Therefore being justified by faith, we have *peace with God* through our Lord Jesus Christ" (Romans

5:1, italics mine). Because of Christ's substitutionary death, this first kind of peace becomes every believer's on the day of salvation. When one reads further in the fifth chapter of Romans, the truth is proclaimed that we are enemies of God (verse 10), but reconciliation was made through the shed blood of Christ to establish this peace, which is accompanied with joy (verse 11). The fall of man made us all guilty and condemned before a holy God, but the perfect sacrifice of His Son mended that broken relationship — putting it back where God originally intended it to be. What wonderful news this is in a world that is in a state of unrest!

Then, there is the peace *of* God. Because of the indwelling person of the Holy Spirit, who takes up residence in every believer on the day of salvation, we can experience this peace — no matter the circumstances. It's available to all Christians, but Christians do not always take advantage of this assurance, sadly. Jesus is the author of the peace imparted to us by the person of the Holy Spirit. Experiencing His peace requires an act of surrender. There's a lot to be said about forgiveness and the weight we tend to carry when we neglect to willingly choose it! As previously mentioned, it's free! Look with me at Philippians 4:6–7: "Be careful for nothing, but in everything by prayer and supplication with thanksgiving let your requests be made known to God. And the *peace of God* which passes all understanding shall keep your hearts and minds through Christ Jesus" (italics mine).

One of my sons had some fears at nighttime early in his childhood. I would habitually read with him from the children's Bible storybook, pray with him, and teach him to pray, and then I told him I loved him as I kissed him good night. He came to know the Lord as Savior at a young age.

One particular evening after I had gone through this familiar routine, turned off the light, and went into another room, I heard the pitter-patter of little feet and a whimper that said, "There's a face on my wall, and the eyes are looking at me!" I grasped his sweet little hand, and he led me back to the room to point it all out. Sure enough, there hung the family photo on one side of the wall and a picture of a clown on the other (which I thought he seemed to love at the time). After I reassured him that each person in the family photo loved him, he replied, "I know them, Mom! It's the clown who is staring at me that I don't like! He has big eyes!"

Inside, I chuckled, but the clown picture came down at his request. I didn't leave the room without acknowledging his fear and letting him know that it could be remedied just by talking to Jesus. It's important to let Him know our fears and then trust Him for His protection. I also took advantage of my son's keen mind and memory by teaching him Psalm 56:3, which says, "What time I am afraid, I will trust in thee." My desire for all my children (and grandchildren) is that they rely on the Lord *first* — and then allow their faith to be strengthened by memorizing His Word.

Have you ever put your trust in someone, believing his or her word was reliable and having no thought of even questioning his or her integrity? Has that trust been violated? David knew where his confidence came from and where to place his trust. "It is better to trust in the Lord than to put confidence in man" (Psalm 118:8). I'm thankful for a lot of faithful, trustworthy friends, but we're all human and we fail. God never fails! His Word is reliable. When we take time to memorize scripture that relates to whatever circumstance we may be going through or areas of our life that need improvement, the Holy Spirit will use it to make us aware of whose we are and what we can be for His glory. We would *all* experience God's peace perpetually if we would just get into the habit of doing that.

"Thou wilt keep him in perfect peace, whose mind is stayed upon thee; because he trusteth in thee" (Isaiah 26:3).

Just recently, I listened again to the reading of John 14. Jesus was teaching His disciples and preparing them for what would take place after His approaching death. It was here that He promised the Comforter (the Holy Spirit), whom He would send to abide with them (and all believers) and teach them the things of the Father. It was during this special time that He said, "Peace I leave with you, my peace I give unto you; not as the world giveth, give I unto you; Let not your heart be troubled, neither let it be afraid" (John 14:27). People will leave us, let us down, and disappoint us. Jesus promised, "I will never leave you, nor forsake you" (Hebrews 13:5). It is my prayer that you know the peace *with* God that comes from giving your heart to Him. It is also my prayer that through the study and memorization of God's Word, you experience the peace *of* God in your daily walk with Him! Peace is not the absence of conflict, but the presence of the mighty Prince of Peace through the conflict.

Prayer
Father, thank You for Your Son, Jesus, who died for me so that I may have eternal life and an open relationship with You. Thank You that peace with God opens the door for the peace of God that is also mine to experience and share with others. May I be a reflection of Your peace today! In the Name of Jesus I pray. Amen.

C H A P T E R   5

Long-Suffering

(The Red Jacket)

Knowing this, that the trying of your faith worketh patience; But let patience have her perfect work, that ye may be perfect and entire, wanting nothing.

—James 1:3–4

For what glory is it, if when ye be buffeted for your faults ye shall take it patiently? But if, when ye do well and suffer for it, ye take it patiently, this is acceptable of God.

—1 Peter 2:20

Because a jacket doubles the wear of the garment, this is what I use to enhance the white dress. Again, red is the coordinating color to represent the shed blood of Christ. When the weather is cold or the temperature drops dramatically, it sure does help to have a jacket on hand! The same is true in life too! At the drop of a hat, the weather can change in a relationship, job surroundings, and life in general. I wish I could say that we can all be free from a little or a lot, but there's quite a bit that we can learn from difficulties. That too takes a lifetime as we learn the ways of the Lord. I read recently the statement that the same boiling water that softens a potato also hardens an egg. There's a characteristic of Christ that shines through when one makes a willful choice to learn from one's mistakes and learn the forgiveness that's also ours through His sacrifice.

Long-suffering is made up of two Greek words, meaning "long" and "tempered." Long-tempered means one has self-restraint when stirred to anger. It paints a picture of someone having a long fuse versus being prone to flying off the handle when a problem arises. There's no retaliation or sense of immediate punishment because one is willing to forbear and show mercy. It is defined as the quality of putting up with others, even when one is severely tired. It gives the appearance of patience even in chaos.

Just think of how our lives would be affected if we displayed long-suffering in regard to family members and individual relationships, where we work, and among those with whom we attend church! It takes a long time to mend a relationship broken by words spoken in the heat of anger. There's a sense of pride that rears its ugly head when we know we're right and someone else is wrong. There's an old proverb that says, "Revenge converts a little right into a great wrong." It is justice gone wild because it follows the rules of the one who is dishing it out. Sights are set on the one seeking vengeance without any consideration whatsoever for the individual on whom it falls. "Dearly beloved, avenge not yourselves, but rather give place unto wrath: for it is written, vengeance is mine; I will repay, saith the Lord" (Romans 12:19). By obeying the Holy Spirit, we can exhibit forgiveness and forbearance toward others instead of striking back against offenses and unkind words.

Though not foreign to anyone who has children, works a forty-hour or more week, or is consumed with the care of an elderly parent or disabled family member (or all the above), each of us will face a time when forbearance is needed. No doubt there are circumstances you could share with me that could be added to this list, for it could grow very long in one lifetime. What I wish to make clear to you (and even remind myself) is the grave realization that, apart from Christ, none of us even comes close to measuring up to this quality. I also wish to encourage you and say that because of the indwelling Holy Spirit, the work is all His! Handing it over to Him is where I have fallen short many times! Someone once said, "I learned a long time ago not to pray for patience because, in answer to my prayer, the Lord sat me right down in the middle of a circumstance where it was a major factor. I didn't like that one bit, so I stopped praying for it!" We may chuckle at the dilemma, but we all start as babies in Christ.

This new faith in Christ will accompany us down many roads—some orchestrated by our own doing but most prepared for us by the Lord as we look to Him for wisdom. The perfecting of our faith comes when we make it a deliberate act of the will to walk humbly before Him and to turn passions into patience. That's what growing up is all about. He will not leave us alone until we learn this valuable lesson of patience. When we get ourselves out of the way and let His long-suffering be brought to the forefront, we may not necessarily notice it in action, but others will. That personal pat on the back is merely evidence of more work to be done to mold us into His image.

Shortly after the birth of our first son, Johnny and I were approached by his parents concerning the bad health of his mother's parents. His grandfather had just retired and almost immediately suffered a stroke that partially paralyzed his right side. To add to his dire situation, his wife (Johnny's grandmother) was diagnosed with Alzheimer's disease. The symptoms surrounding it made it very difficult for his grandfather to handle on his own. Although there were family members living in close proximity to them, their work and personal commitments made it impossible to take on this task of caring for them.

Our family lived in Virginia at the time, so agreeing to care for them meant moving to North Carolina. In addition to being asked if we would consider taking on the responsibility of their care, I had also received the news that I was pregnant with our second child. After speaking personally with his grandfather, Johnny and I realized that this was what the Lord was leading us to do. The advice from close friends in the ministry wasn't always the positive affirmation we desired, but we realized that God's calling of evangelism allowed us to continue no matter the location. We also believed we needed to trust what the Lord told us to do first. We went even without knowing just how long our help would be needed, but we were committed to the end. No two patients with this disease handle the toll it takes on their life alike. Some live a very long time; some don't.

I can recall many a night when the phone would ring, and Daddy Greer (what we so lovingly called Johnny's grandfather) would be frantic that I come right away to see about his wife, Momma Greer. Once again, she had gotten herself into a situation that he just couldn't handle on his own. Here I would go with cleaning supplies in hand, clean linens, clean clothes, or whatever was needed to take care of the situation and get everyone settled into bed once again. Talking an Alzheimer's-ridden lady out of her clothes, into the bath, out of the bath, and back into clean clothes (and again I remind you that I was pregnant) could be quite draining physically, mentally, and emotionally. My lesser virtue is patience anyway! How I depended on the Lord through those years of caregiving! I was also blessed by Daddy Greer and other family members as they lovingly watched this one who was no longer like the wife, mom, or sister they had once known change into someone who could no longer care for herself or even recognize them. This was a twenty-four/seven responsibility that constantly brought me to the throne of grace for the patience and forbearance that I needed, but it was also a time that I would not have changed for anything!

This is simply my story, but I also realize that these pages could not fully contain all that so many others are experiencing even now in caring for spouses, parents, or children who require their personal attention. I have a great admiration for my older sister who is, at the time of this writing, caring for our mom in her own home so Mom will not have to spend her remaining golden years in a rest home. I have friends who are going through cancer treatments and others who have loved ones who've lost the battle over this and other grave extended illnesses. There are so many varied situations we all could find ourselves experiencing. One phone call or knock at the door could test everything within us.

The freedom we enjoy to be able to worship and share our faith, geographically speaking, is so unlike the testimony of others in other parts of the world, where they could be (and are) tortured and killed for even mentioning the sweet name of Jesus! Yet with every twenty-four-hour tick of the clock, they patiently live their lives, faithfully serving and making a difference! We have it so easy in comparison, yet we gripe and complain over the smallest issue.

Personally speaking, I've learned a lot from the stories I've heard (or read) from great men and women of the faith who have shared their experiences on and off the field of service. One in particular is Dr. Helen Roseveare, who was taken prisoner for five months by the rebels in the Congo in 1964 while serving there. After her release, she went back to England for a while and then returned to the Congo to continue the work she believed the Lord had called her to do. *That* is what's so amazing to me! After all the torture she went through during her time of captivity, she decided to go back and serve in the rebuilding of the nation until 1973. Wow! In her book, *Give Me This Mountain*, she tells her story with tremendous candidness and deep conviction regarding her whole journey. Here is what she says as she refers to her roller-coaster experiences.

> As I went up and down from the present peak into the valley between the mountains, I was often shadowed by the very peak I had been enjoying. This I interpreted in a sense of failure and this often led to despair. I felt I was going downwards into the "slough of despond." I see now that I was wrong in this "feeling." The going down was merely an initial moving forward toward the next higher ground, never a going back to base level, so to speak. The shadow was only relative after the brightness of the sun; the valley could provide a period of rest for working our preparatory for the next hard climb. Had I understood this meaning of the sunshine and shadow in my life rather than interpreting my various experiences along life's way as "up" and "down," I might have saved myself many deep heartaches.

This also causes me to reflect on a devotion in *My Utmost for His Highest* by Oswald Chambers called, "The Sphere of Exaltation." Here he alludes to our mountaintop experiences when all is well with our relationship with the Lord. Then, at a moment's notice, we descend. This is what he said.

> The test of our spiritual life is the power to descend; if we have power to rise only, something is wrong. It is a great thing to be on the mount with God, but a man only gets there in order that afterwards he may get down among the devil-possessed and lift them up. The times of exaltation are exceptional, they have their meaning in our life with God, but we must beware lest our spiritual selfishness wants to make them the only time. The mount is not meant to "teach" us anything, it is meant to "make" us something. The moments on the mountaintops are rare moments and they are meant for something in God's purpose.

We who know God's Word can instantly recall the story of Job. It began with a meeting between God and Satan, concerning the scenario of pending results over a man who seemed to have everything going for him. God allowed Satan's intrusion. The one thing the enemy could not touch was his life. Through the course of the loss of children and personal possessions, a body full of sores, and friends with seemingly good advice (in their own eyes), there comes a dialogue with God and Job that takes him all the way back to Creation. The bottom line in helping him consider God's purpose behind his present suffering was self-surrender. Questions came to Job about where he (Job) was when creation was taking place and the great mysteries behind the mighty creatures and the stars that followed. God knew Job's attitude of trust through that. He wanted him to trust Him in all this. I like what John Stott said in his *Through the Bible, Through the Year* devotional, "If it was reasonable for Job to trust God whose wisdom and power have been revealed in the creation, how much more reasonable is it for us to trust the God whose love and justice have been revealed on the cross." Christ, the one who made a relationship with a mighty God possible through Calvary, knows our pain and suffering and relates like no other.

If this serves as an encouragement to any who read it, then I believe the main purpose in this writing was accomplished. I humbly admit I still have a lot to learn in God's plan for my life while conforming me into His Son's image. But this one thing I know: "I can do all things through Christ which strengtheneth me" (Philippians 4:13). I am thankful I know the rest of the story. Romans 8:18 says, "For I reckon that the sufferings of this present time are not worthy to be compared with the glory which shall be revealed in us." There is a promise of a crown for those who endure these present sufferings, and we will have the wonderful privilege of placing it at the feet of Jesus, who walked that road before us and walks now with us. "Fear none of those things which thou shall suffer; behold, the devil shall cast some of you into prison, that ye may be tried; and ye shall have tribulation ten days: be thou faithful unto death, and I will give thee a crown of life" (Revelation 2:10). Stay strong in the Lord, my friend!

Prayer
Father, if we would be honest, we would much rather spend our time on the mountaintop with You. Thank You that You love us more than that and have a far greater goal in mind. When You bring us to the valley, remind us of all we experienced on that mountaintop and grant us Your grace to endure to the end as we obey and serve with thanksgiving and praise, knowing we will look on the face of Jesus, who suffered for us. We offer this prayer in the Name of Jesus. Amen.

CHAPTER 6

Gentleness

(The White Gloves)

Be ye kind one to another, tenderhearted, forgiving one another, even as God for Christ's sake hath forgiven you.

—Ephesians 4:32

Verily I say unto you, Whosoever shall not receive the kingdom of God as a little child, he shall not enter therein. And he took them up in his arms, put his hands upon them, and blessed them.

—Mark 10:15–16

A simple definition of *gentleness* is the quality or state of being gentle; especially mildness of manners or disposition. When looking at the fruit of the Spirit, it is better expressed by the word *kindness*. Gentleness is a conduct of life, especially when dealing with difficult people. Some people just need to be handled with kid gloves. With this in mind, white gloves are used to represent this special fruit. As a reminder too, allow me to reemphasize that long-suffering (patience), gentleness, and goodness all have to do with our relationship with others.

What better example do we have than that of the Son of God? The scripture from the book of Mark at the beginning of this chapter tells the story of Jesus's ministry on earth with His disciples so that they might learn from His teachings as well. Their training, as well as ours, was to prepare them for service after His death and help them to realize that the work to which He now called them would be done with the power of the Holy Spirit. Although the disciples didn't fully understand the whole concept at this particular time, all would become clear after the fulfilling promise of the Comforter (the Holy Spirit), which was to take place after His ascension.

Picture here though a man who had just spent time with the multitudes who were continually flocking around Him in Galilee. He was in Judea, making His way to the cross. The time of day is not mentioned, but there He was, spending time with a different crowd. During this incident, there filtered into his surroundings the Pharisees, whose obvious purpose was to trip him up (Mark 10:2). They hurled a question at him regarding divorce—probably after they had noticed all the families who were in attendance. After all, that was what they enjoyed the most, walking in front of others "to be seen of men" (Matthew 6:5), speaking prayers out loud (mostly with impressive flowery words that were often repeated over and over again). This is found in Matthew 6 when Jesus is giving the model prayer where He specifically teaches His disciples not to be like them. He calls them hypocrites who seek the glory of men (Matthew 6:1–2). Jesus, however, was simply recalling God's absolute standard and intention for marriage without wavering, though His words were not welcomed and were also unfashionable to the culture. The disciples missed this lesson on simple, childlike faith because they wanted to further discuss the issue just as some children were being brought to Him from the crowd. The disciples, along with the crowd, had just witnessed the debate. They saw the children coming toward Jesus, and they tried with all their might to send them away. I love what Jesus said with grave indignation but also with an immediate display of gentleness in Mark 10:14, "But when Jesus saw it, he was much displeased, and said unto them, Suffer the little children to come unto me, and forbid them not; for of such is the kingdom of God."

The very next verse paints the sweetest picture of gentility. Verse 15 points out three significant things. First, He took them into His arms; second, He put His hand on them; and third, He blessed them! Who but a child can sense the gentleness of a hand that touches him or her or can interpret the tone of a voice and excel after a word of commendation and praise? As one of six children whose parents believed in the discipline of not sparing the rod and spoiling the child, I understood when the touch of something other than gentleness was coming my way. I knew the soft and gentle consoling touch as well. I understood the serious tone of a command that bade obedience and appreciated the affirmation of a job well done. Sometimes (or should I actually say all the time), depending on with whom we're dealing, it takes all three of these points to interact with certain individuals whose personalities are a bit harder to deal with. Can you think of someone like that? I believe the Lord brings these people across our path to teach us the wonderful fruit of gentleness.

This brings to mind what I shared in a previous chapter about our time in caring for Mama Greer after she was diagnosed with Alzheimer's disease. Sadly, I never knew her before this had taken place, but I had often heard the stories of how very loving, sweet, and gentle she was. She didn't even come close to having characteristics of one who was always hard to get along with! The effects of the disease created circumstances that only produced irritation.

I remember one particular day when she had slept well past noon and I thought it was time to get her up and dressed for the day. Her eyes were open to give some indication that perhaps she was awake and ready, so I opened the curtains to her room, said good morning, and encouraged her to join the family in enjoying the sunny day. Words started flowing from her mouth the likes of which neither I nor anyone else had heard before from an evident irritation at my invading the peaceful state she had obviously been relishing before I entered the room. I was several months away from delivering our second child and had a toddler who was awaiting my return to him. The to-do list was long, but it seemed even longer now with this reaction. I already shared with you my weakness with patience, but gentleness is put to the test when impatience rears its ugly head as well! Can I please hear an "Amen!"? My one choice here was prayer. As I prayed, the Holy Spirit said to me that perhaps it would be a good idea to pray with Mama Greer as well. As I sat on her side of the bed, took her hand, and rubbed it gently, I said, "Mama Greer, it's such a beautiful day outside. What do you say we pray and ask the Lord to bless it and our time together?"

"Okay, honey" was her reply, and as I asked her to pray, you would not believe the change that took place! She prayed down the glories of heaven. Every step of talking her out of her clothes, into the bath, out of the bath, and back into her clothes flowed much more smoothly than it had some previous days. And what a lesson I learned as well!

As I meditated on this particular fruit of the Spirit and read God's Word with a dependence on the Holy Spirit's guidance on what to share, He brought to mind the relationship of the shepherd to his sheep. We who know the Lord are His sheep, and He is the Great Shepherd. The twenty-third chapter of the book of Psalms is one of the most familiar chapters of the Bible. It is shared at funerals and quoted by individuals in a situation of crisis. I remember quite a few years ago reading the real-life story of an actual shepherd. There is a book entitled *A Shepherd Looks at Psalm 23* by Phillip Keller that does the same. Mr. Keller points out that although David was the author of this Psalm, he is speaking not as the shepherd but as one of the sheep of the flock. Here's what he said.

> He (David) spoke with a strong sense of pride and devotion and admiration. It was as though he boasted literally aloud "Look at who my Shepherd is—my owner—my manager!" The Lord is! After all, he knew from firsthand experience that the lot in life of any particular sheep depended on the type of man who owned it. Some men were gentle, kind, intelligent, brave and selfless in their devotion to their stock. Under one man sheep would struggle, starve and suffer endless hardship. In another shepherd's care they would flourish and thrive contentedly. So, if the Lord is my Shepherd I should know something of His character and understand something of His ability.

Reading this brought to mind a reality show I watched one evening where couples would travel to various places around the world and participate in competitions for a large amount of money, which they would win if they were able to eliminate all other competitors doing the same. Their instructions on this particular foot of the race were to herd sheep into a pen before moving on to the next task. Several of the teams struggled with this because they only realized after a tremendous amount of effort and time that the flailing of arms and loud yells or whistles weren't getting the job done. Sheep would dodge, jolt, scatter, and then come to a sudden halt once the herders did. I just smiled as one smart couple put all of them to shame by accomplishing it almost immediately, simply by gently and quietly working together—one on each side of the herd, directing the sheep exactly to the entrance of the pen with very little effort.

Before David was a king, he was a shepherd. No doubt he spent many nights saying very little and playing his musical instrument to bring calm to a herd that very possibly took the greater part of the day to finally get to where they needed to be and settle for the night. No doubt too this came to mind when he played that same instrument to calm an angry, disturbed King Saul before he occupied the throne himself. Allow me to encourage you to read John 10:1–15. The Lord our Shepherd knows us, His sheep, by name! We deserve judgment because of our sin, but those sins were judged at Calvary. "I am the good Shepherd; the good Shepherd giveth his life for the sheep" (John 10:11).

In showing kindness (gentleness) to others, as stated in Ephesians 4:32, we are a picture of the one who is the epitome of gentleness! How can we forgive? Answer: We can forgive because we've been forgiven! How can we turn the other cheek when we are mistreated, scorned, or persecuted? Answer: We can because the perfect Son of God laid down His life for all humankind!

Prayer

Father, thank You that You know my name and, like a gentle shepherd, You protect me from the enemy and lead me by Your mighty hand. Reveal to me even now how I can, by the power of Your Holy Spirit, show Your gentleness to the ones You bring across my path today so that they can know You too. In the Name of Jesus I pray. Amen.

CHAPTER 7

Goodness

(The White Purse)

And, behold, one came and said unto him, Good Master, what good thing shall I do, that I may have eternal life? And he said unto him, Why callest thou me good? There is none good but one, that is, God; but if thou wilt enter into life, keep the commandments. He saith unto him, Which? Jesus said, Thou shalt do not murder, Thou shalt not commit adultery, Thou shalt not steal, Thou shalt not bear false witness, Honour thy father and thy mother; and, Thou shalt love thy neighbor as thyself. The young man saith unto him, All these things have I kept from my youth up: what lack I yet? Jesus said unto him, If thou wilt be perfect, go and sell that thou hast, and give to the poor, and thou shalt have treasure in heaven; and come and follow me. But when the young man heard that saying, he went away sorrowful; for he had great possessions.

—Matthew 19:16–22

It is so amazing to me how the fruit of the Spirit are intertwined. When one knows the unconditional love of God and realizes the river that flows from within has the capacity to then love someone else, joy is also present. Through the experience of joy, peace is reflected because of our position in Christ by faith. Further still, when God chooses to bring circumstances into our lives to teach us patience, it is accompanied with gentleness toward others simply because we have received that same gentle touch from the Father. Then, who can give more than one who has seen that "every good and perfect gift cometh from the Father" (James 1:17)? In spite of all that we are capable of as His children, He still gives out of an abundant supply. Goodness! That grace upon grace is such that we don't even have to try to earn it, though many spend a lifetime in the struggle.

I think of my grandfather (my father's dad), who was in the hospital, having been diagnosed with colon cancer just shortly before I was to graduate from Bible college. On one particular break, I made a covenant with the Lord that upon my return home for that short period, I would visit him and make sure that he was ready for heaven should he lose the battle with this illness.

I have such fond memories of Granddaddy Johnson. He was a businessman and owned and operated a small trailer park not too far from where we lived. He also bought and sold cattle and horses, and that made up a bit of farming on the land. Nevertheless, he always had time to spend with his grandchildren—no matter how busy he was. He even operated a gas station with a small store, which happened to be right where all six of us children got off the bus after school. How I looked forward to running inside where he would always have candy, soft drinks, or some type of goody ready for us after he got his hug.

When I visited him in his hospital room, he was the frailest I had ever seen him. I was by myself when I walked into the room. After catching up on things that concerned me and my time at school, we fell quiet. I gently picked up his hand and expressed how sorry I was that he had to go through his present ordeal and then asked if he was certain he was headed to heaven if he died this very night.

He put his hand on top of mine and said, "Baby doll, I've tried to live an honest, clean life with the hopes of not doing anyone any wrong. I hope that says enough for me for all my years of hard labor."

My heart was so full that while he was talking, I was crying tears that flowed onto his bed linens. When I could gather my composure, I said, "Granddaddy, if that was what got a man to heaven, you'd be the very first in line! But God's Word says that we must believe that Christ's death on the cross was the payment for our sin and by faith repent and confess our sin, allowing Jesus to take full control of our lives. Being good or doing good things doesn't get it, and I long to see you in heaven one day!"

He didn't pray the prayer of salvation that day, and I returned to school with an even heavier burden. I also prayed and determined in my heart that should the Lord spare his life until I graduated in a month or so, I would see him every day and read to him from the Bible, persevering until he gave his heart to the Lord. Upon graduation day, I was so excited to show my dad and mom the large-print Bible I had purchased to give to him, but they gave me the news that he had passed away the day before they arrived for the ceremony. I could not contain myself. Would I ever see him again?

As I've grown in faith and my walk with the Lord, I realize that we won't always know in this life of those who trusted the message we have been called to give. In the days that followed, I attended his funeral, which had been delayed until after my graduation. After the service, I was seated on a piano stool in the receiving area, oblivious to the people around me because of my grief, wondering if Granddaddy had made peace with God before his death.

A sweet lady seated right beside me spoke to me. When she asked my name and realized I was one of the grandchildren, she said with great excitement, "Oh, you're the one your granddaddy spoke of who was attending a Bible college. He spoke highly of all his grandchildren, and I spent many days with him in the hospital. I want you to know that he gave his heart to Jesus just before he died!" She gave me other details of how it all came about, but the heaviness was lifted from my heart and I expressed to her my gratitude for her sharing that wonderful news with me! In this particular situation, the graciousness of the Lord allowed me to know about my granddaddy's decision. Sadly, I can't say the same about others who have heard the message of salvation that we've been faithful to offer during the years of ministry. I know that Jesus knows, and one day, all will be made clear when we see Him face-to-face.

Goodness is related to kindness and the result is generosity. Edwin Hubel Chapman, who lived from 1814 to 1880, said, "Goodness consists not in the outward things we do, but in the inward." God doesn't merely do things that are good—He is good! Even at our very best, we couldn't come close to His goodness. The Bible word for this is *grace*. Like all the other fruit, we can be avenues of His goodness because of the indwelling Holy Spirit. In our dealings with every person around us, we have the potential to be good but lack the ability apart from Christ. Sometimes, we even have the tendency to overestimate our own goodness, thereby underestimating God's great goodness! The fruit of the Spirit the Bible speaks of here is an eternal goodness that produces an internal goodness in

His children. While goodness is something we *are* through the power of His Holy Spirit, it's also the way we *live* as we allow Him to carry out His work in us. Matthew 12:33–35 says,

> Either make the tree good, and his fruit good, or else make the tree corrupt, and his fruit corrupt; for the tree is known by his fruit. O generation of vipers, how can ye, being evil, speak good things? For out of the abundance of the heart the mouth speaketh. A good man out of the good treasure of the heart bringeth forth good things; and an evil man out of the evil treasure bringeth forth evil things.

I haven't mastered this fruit yet, but God's not finished with me either!

Since the ministry God has given me has been primarily with women, I want to relate to you the story of one who is mentioned in Acts 9. Her name was Tabitha (or Dorcas, in Greek). She was described in verse 36 as a "woman full of good works and almsdeeds which she did." She was sick and had died, and Peter had been traveling through her area when this all took place. He was in the upper chamber with the widows, who were weeping and also showing everyone the coats and garments that Tabitha had made for any who needed them while she was living. They were bearing testimonies to her goodness, which started in her heart and extended to everyone around her. It was during this time that Peter took her hand, lifted her up, and presented her alive to those in the room.

I love the story in the seventh chapter of Luke regarding the unnamed woman who came to Jesus while he was about to enjoy a meal at the home of a Pharisee. Just before this particular scene takes place, Jesus speaks of John the Baptist, who is presently imprisoned. He is approached by some of John's friends, who were witnesses to Jesus's healing of those who were in the crowd and curing many of blindness, deafness, and evil spirits. Here was their question: "Are thou he that should come? Or look we for another?" (Luke 7:20). Jesus's response to them was, "Go your way, and tell John what things ye have seen and heard; how that the blind see, the lame walk, the lepers are cleansed, the deaf hear, the dead are raised, to the poor the gospel is preached. And blessed is he, whosoever shall not be offended in me" (Luke 7:22–23).

For the longest time in my walk with Christ, I didn't fully understand Jesus's response to this question, which was without a doubt delivered to Him by John the Baptist through his friends. But it is still even more amazing to me as I continue to study God's Word how it all comes together perfectly when one reads the whole story, not just a part of it! This forerunner of Christ must have felt he was now rendered useless and ineffective in his calling while in his confinement. The message in Jesus's response was an encouragement of faith that believers need to exercise in performing the work to which Christ calls them, realizing also that there will always be those who on the outside appear religious but in their hearts reject that same message of the gospel we share—especially in the deeds we perform. This took place even here when the miraculous was performed by Jesus. When one reads further, one is told that all who heard Him speak of John the Baptist and saw what He did, including the publicans, believed and were baptized—all except the Pharisees and lawyers! Jesus was confirming the work of His servant while he sat in prison and letting all who heard Him know that the witness of John the Baptist was only just beginning to have an effect on those who would believe.

It was shortly after Jesus's commendations concerning John the Baptist that Simon, who was one of those Pharisees in the crowd, invited Him to his home to eat. You can read verses 24–35 for Jesus's complete message to the crowd. I'm thinking that perhaps even this Pharisee desired to somehow impress Jesus with a bit of his own goodness! Wouldn't you know that just before they were ready to eat, in walked a woman with an alabaster box of ointment. All we know about this one without a name is that she was described as "a sinner" (verse 37) but was privy to Jesus being at Simon's home. What courage and love for Jesus she displayed as she kissed his feet and then washed them with her tears and wiped them with her hair! But she didn't stop there. She then poured the entire contents of the alabaster box, which contained an expensive ointment that probably could have fed her household for a very long time, on Jesus's feet. I'm imagining now the sound of a gasp coming from the host's mouth—just before a lecture on the various ways it could have been used. Luke tells us, though, that his dissatisfaction was now directed at Jesus with accusations that "if he were a prophet, he would have known who and what manner of woman this is that touched him" (Luke 7:39). Jesus proceeded with a story about two people, each who owed their creditor different amounts of money. Both were forgiven their debts. Jesus's question was, "Tell me therefore, which of them will love him [the creditor] the most?" The answer was: "I suppose that he, to whom he forgave the most" (Luke 7:42–43). Jesus then turned to Simon and pointed out all that the woman had done—none of which had even been performed by Simon upon Jesus's entry into his house. She entered the house with a heavy heart in need of forgiveness and left with a life touched by the Savior! Simon witnessed it all. His own goodness now paled in comparison to the goodness lavished on Jesus by this one he had considered simply "a sinner." He even failed to see the goodness of Jesus in forgiving her as he listened to the others who were present in his home, in their piety, simply not believing that Jesus had the power to forgive sins (Luke 7:49). The goodness of God was poured out on the Son of God by one who believed that Jesus was who He said He was. She may not have fully understood all that this anointing meant, but I'm sure she was probably one in a crowd of many who witnessed His death on the cross.

Read Luke 10, the story of Mary and Martha, who had received Jesus in their home for a meal. Mary sat at Jesus's feet, oblivious to everything around her except His voice. Martha, on the other hand, was so caught up in the preparation of the meal that she finally stopped and asked if anyone cared that she was left to herself to get it all done. That would have been me by the way! I too forget the times of worship without realizing that I can worship while I work. Here's Jesus's response though. "Martha, Martha, thou art careful and troubled about many things; But one thing is needful: and Mary hath chosen that good part, which shall not be taken away from her" (Luke 10:41–42).

Don't we all want to be good? We're told from childhood that if we are good, we'll get something special. If we are good, this will happen or that will happen. But Jesus says that even our best is filthy rags. It looks good! It may accomplish something good. It will look good on a résumé or make us feel good. Maybe someone will even say something good about us. But the Lord says, "Being confident of this very thing, that he which hath begun a good work in you will perform it until the day of Jesus Christ" (Philippians 1:6). And my admonition to you is "O taste and see that the Lord is good; blessed is the man that trusteth in him. The young lions do lack, and suffer hunger; but they that seek the Lord shall not want any good thing" (Psalm 34:8–10).

It was during the writing of this chapter that the Lord reminded me of *When God Doesn't Make Sense* by Dr. James Dobson, a Christian psychologist and founder and president of Focus on the Family. Not only has he ministered to individuals, families, and businesses through the work God has given him over the years, but he has been a tremendous blessing to me too, through the radio broadcasts I've listened to, as well as a lot of the books he has authored. In this particular book, he gives one example after another of individuals who have dedicated their lives to the work of the Lord but because of various circumstances along the way were not allowed to see their dreams accomplished or come to fruition. We could also name at least one such story ourselves of various difficulties in our own life or the lives of people we know who have suffered loss, whether it be physical or financial—and the list doesn't just stop there. God has a wonderful plan for each of His children. We fail in a lot of ways when we talk of the goodness of the Lord to also interject that everything is not always coming up roses and that one aspect of the mystery of God is that we won't always have an answer for why He allows things to happen the way they do. To quote Dr. Dobson,

> Unfortunately, many young believers— and some older ones too—do not know that there will be times in every person's life when circumstances don't add up—when God doesn't appear to make sense. This aspect of the Christian faith is not well advertised. We tend to teach new Christians the portions of our theology that are attractive to a secular mind.

I like what the Lord states through Jeremiah, who is known as "the weeping prophet": "For I know the plans

I have for you, declares the Lord, plans to prosper you and not to harm you, plans to give you hope and a future" (Jeremiah 29:11 NIV). Dr. Dobson goes on to say in summary, "God's plan is wonderful because anything in harmony with His will ultimately 'works for the good of those who love him, who have been called according to his purpose'" (Romans 8:28).

Recently I've spent a lot of time in Psalm 34 and am hoping to one day have it committed to memory. The more I witness the Lord's goodness to me, the more I want others to be a recipient of His goodness through me. I'm guilty of hoarding His goodness at times. I'm also guilty of questioning His goodness when things don't go the way I think they should. But as you read in the opening verse from Luke 6, we can never outgive Him. The late husband of Elizabeth Elliott said it this way: "A man (or woman) is no fool to give what he/she cannot keep, to gain what they cannot lose." "Little is much when God is in it" (as is the title of the song I love.) The Lord so graciously takes what we do in His name, by His power, with His direction and multiplies it His way. I can only end this chapter this way because there is so much more to learn regarding His goodness by sharing with you what Johnny and I have said so many times since the day the Lord brought us together: "The Lord is good to Johnny and Wanda!" It's not because we deserve it, but because He wants us to be that channel through which others can also be lavished with His goodness.

"Do not lay up for yourselves treasures on earth, where moth and rust destroy, and where thieves break in and steal; but lay up for yourselves treasures in heaven, where moth nor rust corrupt and where thieves do not break in and steal. For where your treasure is, there your heart will be also" (Matthew 6:19). One of my favorite verses is "Give, and it shall be given unto you, good measure, pressed down, and shaken together, and running over, shall men give into your bosom. For with the same measure ye mete, withal it shall be measured to you again" (Luke 6:38).

Prayer

Lord Jesus, I confess to You today that I need to be reminded by You that in me there is nothing good except for the goodness of the Lord. I realize the futility of anything that may seem good in my own eyes. Forgive me for doubting You when things don't always go the way I would like. Thank you for your salvation and the very presence of God through the Holy Spirit that allows me to be the channel through which Your goodness can be received by others. I want to worship You more. I want to trust You more. May Your eternal goodness produce an internal goodness in me every day. In the Name of Jesus I pray. Amen.

CHAPTER 8

Faith

(The Gold Watch)

It is of the Lord's mercies that we are not consumed, because his compassions fail not. They are new every morning; great is thy faithfulness.

—Lamentations 3:22–23

Let a man so account of us, as of the ministers of Christ, and stewards of the mysteries of God. Moreover it is required in stewards, that a man be found faithful.

—1 Corinthians 4:1–2

Fear none of those things which thou shalt suffer; behold, the devil shall cast some of you into prison, that ye may be tried; and ye shall have tribulation ten days: be thou faithful unto death, and I will give thee a crown of life.

—Revelation 2:10

An important item in a woman's wardrobe is her watch. I remember a long time ago owning one with bands of various colors that were interchangeable so as to match an outfit. Others probably own a gold or silver one to simplify things a bit. When talking about this particular fruit of the Spirit, however, a gold watch represents faith. Gold, of course, stands for purity in our walk of faith. You're probably wondering what this item has to do with faith at all. Let me explain! Dr. Billy Graham is known for saying it this way: "It is the life of our time that is more important than the time of our life." (This was originally said by Abraham Lincoln.) It is not the saving faith we're going to look at during this time of our study, but the faithfulness of a life that is yielded to Christ once we accept His great salvation. Remember that love, joy, and peace characterize our relationship with God; long-suffering (patience), goodness, and meekness characterize our relationship with others; and finally, faith, gentleness, and temperance (self-control) relate to the mastery of our own selves. It begins with faith — and, depending on how we live this life under the guidance of the Holy Spirit, it ends in faith.

Now begins the process of knowing Christ and becoming more like Him as we spend time in His Word. The Bible is our own personal love letter from God the Father, with promises we can claim as our very own because we serve a faithful God. Second Timothy 2:13 says, "If we believe not, yet he abideth faithful: he cannot deny himself."

When I was working as a member of a team missionary group during my time in the Bible Institute, our first activity during the week, after a time of devotions with the chaplain of the campground where we served, was with children. We performed with puppets and music and then spent time explaining how they could know Christ as Savior. It's still amazing to me to this day how the Holy

Spirit speaks to people of all ages about their need for Christ. By faith, we give the gospel plan of salvation, and by faith, we trust the work that He does in their hearts beyond their commitment. When we finished the time of prayer with these young ones, we would then have them hold up their hand with all five fingers spread out and ask them to repeat after us: "I will never leave you!" They repeated each word back to us as they pointed from the thumb to the pinkie in repetition so as to remind them of the Lord's faithfulness to them in their walk with Him.

All of us start our walk as newborn babes in Christ and grow as we discover God's faithfulness while spending time with Him. It's not His desire that we stay babies but that we find strength and encouragement in who He is and what He longs to do through His children who develop a keen ear to the Holy Spirit, who is changing us into His likeness. "Heaven and earth shall pass away, but my words shall not pass away" (Matthew 24:35). I'm also blessed by the fact of His faithfulness that extends not only to myself and those whom Johnny and I have the privilege of giving the gospel to in this great work of evangelism but also to my family and extended family! "For the Lord is good; his mercy is everlasting; and his truth endureth to all generations" (Psalm 100:5).

We've often heard the testimony of those who came to know the Lord late in life and regret not having done it sooner. Then there have been those whose lives were changed while in their youth though they didn't really walk in fellowship with the Lord until later in life. I'm thankful I serve a God of second chances! As a matter of fact, His forgiveness is boundless beyond even the second chance. "See then that ye walk circumspectly, not as fools, but as wise; Redeeming the time, because the days are evil" (Ephesians 5:15–16). Let's get to it *now*! I believe while there is air in our lungs, it's never too late to grow in the life of faith. We're also urged to go and tell others of this great news and make this appeal: "For he saith, I have heard thee in a time accepted, and in the day of salvation have I succoured thee: behold, now is the accepted time; behold, now is the day of salvation" (2 Corinthians 6:2).

We begin the life of faith by spending time before the Lord in His Word every day and in corporate worship with other believers. In my daily and personal devotional time, the core worship begins with prayer and intercessions for others, His Word (I focus on various topics or reading through it completely), and various devotionals that have been written by godly men and women (all with different topics of study). I have also incorporated hymns that include the stories behind them. I love the old hymns of the faith!

One in particular is "Great Is thy Faithfulness," written by Thomas Chisholm. He lived a simple, humble life. Although he did not complete high school, he somehow managed to become a teacher—at the young age of sixteen—in the same small country school he had attended. After his salvation, he was later ordained as a Methodist preacher and enjoyed writing poems. "Great Is Thy Faithfulness" seemed to be one of his and his readers' most favorite of all. Here is what he had to say about God's faithfulness in his life before he passed away in 1960.

> My income has never been large at any time in the earlier years which has followed me on until now. But I must not fail to record here the unfailing faithfulness of a covenant-keeping God and that He has given me many wonderful displays of His providing care which have filled me with astonishing gratefulness. (Osbeck 1990)

There is great inspiration and encouragement in the testimonies of men and women of the faith!

I made the decision to go to Liberty University, and I was surrounded by guys and gals in an environment where the study of God's Word was the core, sat under men and women professors whose lives were dedicated to the training of "young champions for Christ" (as was the motto of the late Dr. Jerry Falwell, founder), and witnessed the call of God on individuals whom I was privileged to know. Some thirty-plus years later, there are some who have left the call because of various circumstances. Personally, I had no intention of attending higher education until I visited a high school girlfriend who had attended Liberty right after high school graduation. I was assistant manager of a ladies' dress shop, had a car that was paid for, and was considering moving into a place of my own. On this particular weekend of visitation, I was almost immediately affected by the spirit and enthusiasm of the kids on campus. I saw a change in my friend as well and was brought to my knees when the Holy Spirit kept saying to me, "If you want to really know what God's direction is for your life and if you want to marry a man who is sold out for the Lord, then this is where you need to be!" I vividly remember falling down beside the bed in the hotel room where we stayed and asking my friend to pray with me concerning this matter. I knew I needed to obey the Lord, but the challenge was in convincing my parents of the same. Upon returning home, I spent time in prayer continually, waiting for the right moment to bring this matter to them. I sought the confirmation of their blessing upon my decision, but more than that, I wanted to present it to them with a confidence that had the very hand of God behind it.

I remember reading Luke 9:62, which says, "And Jesus said unto him, No man, having put his hand to the plough, and looking back, is fit for the kingdom of God."

In the previous verses, Jesus was calling individuals to follow Him but was given one excuse after another as to why they couldn't do so. There was even one who said he would follow Him, but it wouldn't be automatically because of a death in his family. My heart's desire was to obey Him instantly—although my dad and mom thought I had lost my mind. I was hammered with many questions (that no doubt I considered also), such as: How will you pay for this? You know you'll have to turn around and sell the car that is paid off, right? What will you study? What? Where? Why? There was a pretty involved list of questions. The next statement was the critical one though. It led me to realize they knew I was headstrong on this decision to go, but they were making one last-ditch effort to stop me in my tracks. They said. "You do realize that once you decide on this we can't help you financially. There's no way we can afford to put six children through college, so you're on your own." I would be lying if I said that these words constantly ringing in my ears in the days to follow didn't frighten me a bit! What they did do though was push me toward a closer walk with the Lord and brought about a greater dependence on Him that has not been without lessons of faith that would take from now until Jesus's return to exhaust their telling! I would receive letters in the mailbox, accompanied by checks of small amounts to great amounts, from people I knew and people I will probably never meet in this lifetime.

I clearly remember making my way to the financial office upon my graduation with a bill in hand, praying all the way there that the Lord would help me explain how I would pay it off. Consequently, after I had waited a moment for the clerk to fill me in on what was required for final payment, she returned to the window to say, "I'm sorry, Wanda, but our records show that your bill has been paid in full!"

Only one word came out of my mouth, "How?"

Her simple reply was, "The one who took care of this on your behalf wishes to remain anonymous!"

What? I walked away without even remembering if I said thank you, have a good day, or anything else. All I could do was find the closest chair to help me off my buckling legs and spend a few tearful moments in praise before the Lord. It humbled me greatly. It was God's affirmation to me of His great faithfulness. It created in me a greater desire to serve Him faithfully too. His call on my life—whatever and wherever and however He leads—is forever accompanied by the evidence of His great faithfulness. Like Paul, it behooves me to "press toward the mark" (Philippians 3:14).

As I have previously stated, *My Utmost for His Highest*, a devotional by Oswald Chambers, is a tool I've used repeatedly over the years. In speaking of the call of God in the lives of His children, he says this:

> Remember the need is not the call—the need is the opportunity to exercise the call. The call is to be faithful to the ministry you received when you were in true fellowship with the Father. You must be sensitive to God's call, which means it may require ignoring demands for service in other areas. God's call is the **BEST**—let's not choose second best.

I didn't fully understand the exact vocation at the time of God's call on my life as a young teenager.

After graduating from the Bible Institute, meeting and marrying the man who was sold out to also serve the Lord, and trusting the Lord's provision these thirty-five years in this work of evangelism that we share as a couple, I stand in awe of His faithfulness to me and long to serve Him faithfully until He returns or chooses to bring me home by way of physical death. What I do understand is this: "But without faith it is impossible to please Him; for he that cometh to God must believe that He is, and that He rewards them that diligently seek Him" (Hebrews 11:6). It is my desire to please Him. I'm realizing more and more as the years are added to my life that "we walk by faith not by sight" (2 Corinthians 5:7). Does that mean I have not faltered and failed along the way? No! He forgives, restores, strengthens, supplies, and continues to use His children—most of the time in spite of us! "Faithful is He that calleth you, who also will do it" (1 Thessalonians 5:24).

According to Galatians 2:20, even the faith we exercise is not our own: "I am crucified with Christ: nevertheless I live; yet not I, but Christ liveth in me: and the life which I now live in the flesh I live by the faith of the Son of God, who loved me, and gave Himself for me." I'd like to conclude with these verses from the great hymn "Great Is Thy Faithfulness." Be blessed by it, and begin your walk of faith *now*! "I must work the works of Him who sent me while it is day; the night cometh when no man can work" (John 9:4).

Great Is Thy Faithfulness
by Thomas Chisholm

Great is thy faithfulness, O God my Father!
There is no shadow of turning with Thee.
Thou changest not; Thy compassions, they fail not.
As Thou hast been Thou forever wilt be.

Summer and winter, and springtime and harvest
Sun, moon and stars in their courses above.
Join with all nature in manifold witness
To Thy great faithfulness, mercy and love.

Pardon for sin and a peace that endureth,
Thine own dear presence to cheer and to guide.
Strength for today and bright hope for tomorrow.
Blessings all mine, with ten thousand beside.

Chorus
Great is Thy faithfulness! Great is Thy faithfulness!
Morning by morning new mercies I see.
All I have needed Thy hand hath provided.
Great is Thy faithfulness, Lord, unto me.

Prayer
Great is Thy faithfulness, dear Lord! Our hearts could sing this song before You today and every day in devotion and worship to a God who calls us and provides for us so that we may do the work as others also trust Your faithfulness. We confess that, though our heart longs to trust You, we are prone to wander and sometimes miss out on all that You long for us to do. Forgive us and complete your work in us we pray in the Name of Jesus. Amen.

CHAPTER 9

Meekness

(The Red Hat)

Blessed are the meek; for they shall inherit the earth.
— Matthew 5:5

Likewise, ye wives, be in subjection to your own husbands; that, if any obey not the word, they also may without the word be won by the conversation of the wives; While they behold your chaste conversation coupled with fear. Whose adorning let it not be that outward adorning of plaiting the hair, and of wearing of gold, or of putting on of apparel; But let it be the hidden man of the heart, in that which is not corruptible, even the ornament of a meek and quiet spirit, which is in the sight of God of great price.
— 1 Peter 3:1–4

Brethren, if a man be overtaken in a fault, ye which are spiritual, restore such an one in the spirit of meekness; considering thyself, lest thou also be tempted.
— Galatians 6:1

When collecting the items needed for this visual teaching on the fruit of the Spirit, I found myself lacking a hat. It had to be red — just like the jacket and shoes — to represent the shed blood of Christ. I never thought I had the right shaped head to wear one, but I've seen so many women who can don a hat beautifully. I happened to be at church on one particular day when I was approached by a lady who had a red hat in hand. She had gotten word of my search for one and said that she used to be a member of the "Red Hat Club" and was no longer in need of it. She graciously offered it to me to keep. I'd always admired her since coming to this church. I watched her, along with several others, as she cleaned and took special care to make sure our whole church — from the classrooms, hallways, restrooms, and sanctuary — had a testimony to all who entered of honor to our Lord in its appearance. I think of her every time I speak to a group of women. I admire her meekness. How fitting that this would be the story I could share when speaking of this particular fruit as well.

There are several definitions of the word *meekness*. It means yielded, humble, compliant, and submissive. The outward display of meekness is like that of gentleness and kindness, although this is the second fruit that is a reflection of our mastery over our own selves. And, like I've said before, I'm learning more and more how all the fruit work together in fashioning us into the image of Christ. I've heard it said like this by quite a few preachers and teachers of the Word, "Meekness is not weakness, but strength under the control of the Holy Spirit."

There is a presence of a steady calm in the one who strives to exercise this fruit of meekness. No, it doesn't mean that everything surrounding you is cool, calm, and collected. It is a resignation to the one who has been given full trust to have complete control in that situation. There's no sign of laziness but of waiting in the presence of God with a confidence that chooses not to concede to the surrounding voices. Instead, we deliberately run to that quiet place where we listen solely to the voice of the Spirit, saying, "This is the way. Walk ye in it."

I can look back now and see the strict discipline of my father and mother, requiring me to say, "Yes, ma'am," and "No, ma'am," and "Please" and "Thank you," along with showing respect to older people by using titles such as "Mr. and Mrs." when addressing them verbally. All this is related to putting someone else above yourself with simple courtesies. It puts one in submission to another and teaches an honorable act of even putting the other person above oneself. I've also tried to teach the same to my own children. How much more peaceful things are in the home and workplace when this respect is displayed! We lose this respect when we start comparing our lives with the next person's or have a false view of another's prosperity compared to our own. On the other side of the coin, we may also fret if we witness the leniency shown when we see someone possibly getting by with repeatedly doing evil things while we strive to do what's right. Psalm 37 encourages us to trust in the Lord, to delight ourselves in the Lord, and to commit our way to Him and rest in Him. The *resting* reflects an outward meekness that the Lord uses to teach us, and He uses it to reach others.

The hat is a symbol of meekness. It began with African rituals and was carried into America by African slaves. It was a strong symbol of the ability to triumph over the hardships they had experienced. There was even a hat etiquette established in sort of an unofficial way, although it is said that it was taken very seriously. Here are a few of the rules of any and all who wore a hat, especially in church, were expected to follow. No hat brim should be wider than the shoulders. It should not be darker than the shoes that were worn with the outfit and had to match said outfit. One was not to touch or even borrow one that belonged to someone else. The hat would eventually be passed down to a daughter or granddaughter.

In the everyday situations of home and the work place, the use of head coverings were for protection, bodily warmth, or as a public fashion statement. It was proper for men to remove their hat when entering a public place or place of worship. It showed grave disrespect if not removed during prayer. To show respect in public, the man would tip his hat when in the presence of a woman or dignitary. Not removing the helmet or visor during medieval days to identify yourself could mean immediate death!

God's house is a place of refuge for many. As Christians find fellowship with those of like faith, with the foundation of their faith based on the truths of God's Word, it is appropriate for women to cover their heads. It became a visual symbol of meekness and humility before the One they worshiped. The fashionable hats of everyday life would change simply by adding a flower, feather or ribbon when it was time to enter the place of worship with the sole purpose of perhaps catching God's eye. This was their way of being assured that their deepest prayer would be heard.

I also related this information with that given by Paul when he spoke of head coverings. "Every man praying or prophesying, having his head covered, dishonoreth his head. But every woman that prayeth or prophesieth with her head uncovered dishonoreth her head: for that is even all one as if she were shaven" (1 Corinthians 11:4–5). He goes on further in the chapter to say that the woman was made for the man and the man for God, showing an order of submission. Take time to reread what Peter said in the scripture given at the beginning of this chapter. Along with submission—which is a wonderful act of devotion and love shown first and foremost to our heavenly Father— meekness is the spirit in which we learn to develop discipline and in which by faith, we have the privilege to lead someone else to Christ.

Moses is an example of meekness, for it says in Numbers 12:3, "Now the man Moses was very meek, above all the men which were upon the face of the earth." Go back, though, and read the verses beforehand where the story is told about Miriam and Aaron being none too complimentary of the Ethiopian woman that Moses had married. They made this quite public and even disrespected his position while coming up with the idea that perhaps Moses wasn't the only one to whom the Lord spoke. The rest of the story proved them to be right, for the Lord did appear with words of chastisement to them both, coupled with Miriam being struck with leprosy. Aaron was brought to his knees with a spirit of conviction and found himself begging Moses to intercede for them before the Lord. Moses displayed a spirit of meekness toward them and sincerely prayed for the Lord's intervention on their behalf.

I believe that we can take all too lightly the disrespect we show at times to God's man who stands in the pulpit even today. I've had to ask the Lord's forgiveness myself when pricked in my heart regarding a word spoken out of season or when voicing an honest opinion. God helps us to remember our place in praying for that preacher or evangelist who has been called by Him in filling the task of shepherding His people and proclaiming the good news of salvation!

I can remember in the early years of this ministry the comments made by meaningful, yet insensitive, pastors to my husband. They thought that Johnny looked too young to be doing this kind of work — as if a youthful appearance had anything to do with God's calling on one's life. He, in his meekness, never took it as seriously as I. It just brought back painful memories for me of church business meetings gone awry or disgruntled members who weren't always in favor of particular decisions made by the leadership. I realize more now than ever how so very important it is to pray for all those in leadership positions.

Also at the top of my prayer list are those who — for one reason or another — fall from the faith. We are instructed by Paul to "restore such an one in the spirit of meekness; considering thyself, lest thou also be tempted" (Galatians 6:1). Several things come into play when we don't follow this very wise instruction. We begin to think of ourselves as being better than someone else. That opens the door to deception, doesn't it? Then, there begins the routine of comparing ourselves with someone else, forgetting that the one model whom we should be concerned about is Jesus! Who can be that perfect? Yet, He is the one we should strive to be like. And lastly, we lose sight of our own sin when we see the weakness of another and forget to realize that sooner or later we reap what we sow. Whenever you get to feeling really good about yourself, just take time to read the sixth chapter of Galatians — and prepare to be humbled! "Wherefore let him that thinketh he standeth take heed lest he fall" (1 Corinthians 10:12).

One of the beatitudes of Jesus, given in Matthew 5:5, says, "Blessed are the meek, for they shall inherit the earth." These words came from the one who would very soon be offering Himself as the sacrifice for the sins of the world. He was quoting from Isaiah and preparing His disciples for the ministry they would have following His death.

> The Spirit of the Lord God is upon me; because the Lord hath anointed me to preach good tidings unto the meek; he hath sent me to bind up the brokenhearted, to proclaim liberty to the captives, and the opening of the prison to them

that are bound; To proclaim the acceptable year of the Lord, and the day of vengeance of our God; to comfort all that mourn. (Isaiah 61:1–2)

During Isaiah's time, the Spirit of the Lord came upon people temporarily. After Jesus's death, there was the promise of the Comforter, in the person of the Holy Spirit. Jesus was teaching all those there who followed Him of a relationship with the Father, which is also displayed in the way we serve our fellow humans. Many will not believe. There will be trials and tribulations, and we may even be imprisoned for our belief in Him, but the presence of the wicked is temporary.

The children of Israel needed to exercise this spirit of meekness as they awaited their Deliverer, and so do we. Jesus says that we are "blessed"—meaning "perfectly happy." Following the will of the Lord in meekness— taking the good with the bad—results in "inheriting the earth." His kingdom will be—*and is*—our kingdom! What a great expectation! We should be fervent in our efforts to visit the prisoners, bear the burdens of our fellow humans, and proclaim this liberty that is ours in Christ! Jesus is coming again. It could be today!

Prayer
Father, forgive us when we dishonor You by dishonoring those You have put in authority over us. Thank You for this blessed life that is ours! Thank You for the privilege that is also ours to go into prisons and even across the road to share the liberty we possess through Christ so that others may know it as well. As we worship and serve You in the spirit of meekness, may we also serve our fellow humans until You come. In the Name of Jesus we make this prayer. Amen.

CHAPTER 10

Temperance

(The Girdle / Hair Spray)

And every man that striveth for the mastery is temperate in all things. Now they do it to obtain a corruptible crown; but we an incorruptible. I therefore so run, not as uncertainly; so fight I, not as one that beateth the air: But I keep under my body, and bring it into subjection; lest by any means, when I have preached to others, I myself should be a castaway.

—1 Corinthians 9:25–27

What? Know ye not that your body is the temple of the Holy Ghost which is in you, which ye have of God, and ye are not your own? For ye are bought with a price; therefore glorify God in your body, and in your spirit, which are God's.

—1 Corinthians 6:19–20

I can almost see the expression on your face as you ask, "Girdle? Hair spray? What?" I was pretty amused the first time I saw this being taught by Mrs. Celeste Wemp at a ladies' retreat. She didn't have a girdle to prove her point, but all she had to do was mention it and almost everyone in the room knew exactly what she meant. I was in my early twenties, and wearing a girdle was not my forte — nor was it needful! Now some thirty-five-plus years later, we have at our disposal the great invention of Spanx — that innovative lingerie addition to many a woman's wardrobe that helps hold things in place. Forget the fact that with just a bit of discipline and moderation in eating habits and exercise, there would be no need for it at all. I speak to myself first and foremost!

The topic of weight control and weight loss is a very touchy one for men and women alike. Why? Because if we are all honest with ourselves and each other, we will admit the lack of personal discipline is a hard pill to swallow! To avoid all controversy, I resort to a bottle of *extrahold* hair spray in my travels because the concept is the same. After all, it has been used by men and women alike to hold their hair in place and sure comes in handy on an exceptionally windy day!

There are several definitions to temperance: self-control; restraint over one's impulses, emotions, or desires; moderation in actions; abstinence from intoxicating drink (intoxication means "out of control" — and it can come from anger); and finally, the capacity to keep words, emotions, and actions under personal guard. Wow, what a list! Should you want to put the book down right now, I would understand, but please *hang* with me just a few minutes more and we can both discover that, although most of us struggle in attaining victory in areas of our life where temperance is involved, victory *is* just a prayer away. As

Romans 8:37 says, "Nay, in all these things we are more than conquerors through Him that loved us."

A new year has begun as I write this chapter. Oh, the timing of the Lord for me personally! With a new year comes the resolution to lose weight, save more money, make personal changes in relationships, set different goals that affect careers, and so on. The list is wide and varied. Some resolutions are made with grave sincerity while most are made simply because it's the thing to do. I confess to you that I have even begun a regimen of walking three miles a day on my treadmill to lose weight and firm my body a bit. It wasn't a New Year's resolution but a decision I made upon starting a chapter that deals with self-control. Every time I would try to sit down and write, the Lord just kept dealing with me concerning areas that I needed to deal with before He could sincerely use anything I had for the reader.

When speaking of temperance (or self-control) as the last fruit of the Spirit, like all the other fruit, it behooves us to fall prostrate before the Lord as we allow Him to reveal the true state of our heart. In a world that encourages us to get all the gusto we can and do what feels good, there are issues that we and our loved ones face on a daily basis, and apart from Christ and the power of His Holy Spirit, we're left frantically moving from one whim to the next with hopes of finally discovering the one thing that brings total satisfaction. "And every man that striveth for the mastery is temperate in all things. Now they do it to obtain a corruptible crown; but we an incorruptible" (1 Corinthians 9:25). According to the various definitions mentioned earlier, it's plain to see that until we come face-to-face with the bottom-line truth that the origin of most battles is in the heart and the mind, the victory will come later rather than sooner. I can clearly remember hearing my own father saying to me one day, "I sure hope your strong will and stubbornness will work to your advantage one of these days because right now, it's getting you in real trouble!" I loved that man! He went to be with Jesus in 2004. He was so gentle and wise. I wish I could have just one moment more with him even now to reminisce over things I learned from his strong leadership and confess to him the battles lost because I failed to take his advice to heart.

Again, let's be honest with ourselves. We all know what it looks like when the flesh is in control and our words, actions, and lack of respect for the feelings of others dominate. Look once again at Galatians 5:19–21. The list is long and ugly and makes up what the flesh is apart from Christ. Sadder still is the picture of one who proclaims Christ as Savior and brings shame to His Name because he or she refuses to "crucify the flesh with the affections and lusts" (Galatians 5:24). The verses that follow this remind us that we are to walk in the Spirit, we are not to desire vainglory, nor are we to provoke or be envious of someone else. The verses I chose to head this chapter are grave reminders of how to maintain the temple where the Holy Spirit dwells. Paul even gave an illustration in 1 Corinthians of running a race during his particular time in history and the disciplines he endured to make it to the finish line.

I am reminded of my own involvement in sports during high school when I played softball. The days spent in practice before a game were excruciating; we ran laps and swung the bat as the coach would pitch ball after ball after ball until she was pleased with the result of our swing. I thought my arm would literally fall off! It had to stay attached though, because the next step involved throwing the ball from base to base and to everyone in the outfield until we heard the final whistle of approval (or until we had to give the field to the guys for their practice time).

Paul also gives the example of a fighter. With gloves on and a determination to train, eat, and sleep properly and not be swayed from what it takes to receive the prize, he or she gives very little thought to throwing in the towel or quitting. The battle is won first in the preparation and training, but the prize is won when with confidence we execute everything we learned from the training when tested. We made sacrifices because we fixed our eyes on the prize. "I beseech you therefore, brethren, by the mercies of God, that ye present your bodies a living sacrifice, holy, acceptable unto God, which is your reasonable service. And be not conformed to this world; but be ye transformed by the renewing of your mind, that ye may prove what is that good, and acceptable, and perfect, will of God" (Romans 12:1–2).

There are a lot of stories I could share from my own personal experiences since I gave my heart to Jesus as a young girl regarding this topic of temperance. I'm realizing more and more as I grow in Christ that self-control has nothing at all to do with "self"; rather it is complete reliance on the Holy Spirit's control of my life. Firsthand experience has shown me too many times the hurt I can bring to someone else by speaking before thinking or failing to be discreet even though what I said was the truth. Many financial miseries have come my way because of impulse buying or pampering wants over needs. I've reacted in situations where if I had taken only a few minutes more to allow myself to hear the sweet, small voice of the Holy Spirit in the matter, I could have responded instead.

I'm reminded of a situation when my first two sons were small. They had been playing outside for what seemed to be hours. I had prepared dinner, and it was time for a bath. What broke loose in the moments to come threw me for a loop because one of those two sons let me know immediately that he wasn't ready to come in. He let me (and the whole neighborhood) know in high volume his feelings on the matter. Somehow I coaxed him from the open air and into the house, hoping he would hear my consolations and rationale concerning his adamant protest. He went kicking and screaming into the warm, sudsy water, leaving me wetter than he was! Then, at my wit's end, I left him flailing as I swung back my head and started singing, "Happy day! Happy day! When Jesus washed my sins away! He taught me how to watch and pray and live rejoicing every day! Happy day! Happy day! When Jesus washed my sins away" (words by Phillip Doddridge). There was silence in the room—no crying. Stillness prevailed, and his eyes were as wide as saucers. This child probably thought his mother had lost her mind! The irony of it all was full cooperation for the remainder of bath time. The other son, who was waiting for his turn in the tub, witnessed the whole situation and with laughter said, "Hey, Mom, I get it! Jesus washes our sins away, but Mom washes the dirt away!" I could have gotten just as upset as this little guy and even exercised my authority as his parent in a different manner as well.

There was a different lesson to be learned here—a lesson for my sons *and* a lesson for me. It's all in how we respond. I'm still learning. No two situations are the same when it comes to the test of exercising temperance. I like what Johnny shared with a group of young people years ago in the early days of our marriage. He encouraged them to see what God's Word had to say regarding their own personal weaknesses. Whether it was anger, lying, or bad language, they should find a verse that pertained to it and memorize it. We should be doing that as adults too! The bent of human nature is ugly, no matter the age. The promises of God never change, nor does He lie. The Holy Spirit is about changing us into His wonderful image, but we have to admit the weakness and allow Him to turn it into strength.

From the time our eyes open in a new day until the time we close them at night, we make choices. The people with whom we interact on a daily basis can influence our choices also, if we allow them. When my children were growing up, the Lord showed me that my attitude toward them before sending them off to school could either make or break their day. I also learned by faith to commit their day under the leadership of others to my heavenly Father and pray that their choices would be in accordance with what they were taught at home.

Faith is indeed the bottom-line lesson when it comes to our temperaments or *moods*. I like what Oswald Chambers in *My Utmost for His Highest* had to say about moods in one devotional entitled, "Taking Possession of Our Own Souls." The scripture verse is Luke 21:19. It says, "By your patience possess your souls." On the shorter end, here's what he had to say:

> When a person is born again, there is a period of time when he does not have the same vitality in his thinking or reasoning that he previously had. We must learn to express this new life within us, which comes by forming the mind of Christ. Luke 21:19 means that we take possession of our souls through patience. We fail because we are ignorant of the way God has made us, and we blame things on the devil that are actually the result of our own undisciplined natures. Just think what we could be when we are awakened to the truth! We have to pick ourselves up by the back of the neck and shake ourselves; then we will find that we can do what we believed we were unable to do. The problem that most

of us are cursed with is simply that we won't. The Christian life is one of spiritual courage and determination lived out in our flesh.

This is from the updated edition, which is written in today's language. And to that I will add that it is all accomplished through the realization of the power of the mighty Holy Spirit in us! "Therefore if any man be in Christ, he is a new creation: old things are passed away, behold, all things are become new" (2 Corinthians 5:17). Every day merits us the opportunity to change our moods, our words, and our walk. It's an incorruptible crown that we will have the awesome privilege of placing at the feet of Jesus. "Every man who strives for the mastery is temperate *in all things*" (1 Corinthians 9:25 — italics mine).

Prayer
Father, thank You for teaching us that attaining self-control has very little to do with our own "self" but everything to do with our yielded surrender to Your sweet Holy Spirit. Guide us in our choices. Allow that our mood, our words, and our walk be such as brings glory to Your name. As we strive to become more like You, show us the area of our life where we need to make the changes. Thank You for loving us for who we are. May others see Jesus in us at home, in the workplace, and in our church and our community. We pray these things in the Name of Jesus. Amen.

C H A P T E R   1 1

The Word of God

(The Mirror)

For if any be a hearer of the word, and not a doer, he is like unto a man beholding his natural face in a glass: For he beholdeth himself, and goeth his way, and straightway forgetteth what manner of man he was.

—James 1:23–24

Jesus saith unto him, Have I been so long time with you, and yet hast thou not known me, Phillip? He that hath seen me hath seen the Father; and how sayest thou then, show us the Father? Believest thou not that I am in the Father, and the Father in me? The words that I speak unto you I speak not of myself: but the Father that dwelleth in me, he doeth the works. Believe me that I am in the Father, and the Father in me; or else believe me for the very works' sake.

—John 14:9–11

Should a man see only popularity, he becomes a mirror, reflecting whatever needs to be reflected to gain acceptance. Should a man see only power, he becomes a wolf—prowling, hunting, and stalking the elusive game. Should a man see only pleasure, he becomes a carnival thrill-seeker, alive only in bright lights, wild rides, and titillating entertainment. He is driven only by passion, willing to sell his soul if need be for one more rush, one more race of the pulse, one more sideshow that will take him away from the real world of promises broken and commitments to keep. Seekers of popularity, power and pleasure. The end result is the same: painful unfulfillment. Only in seeing his Maker does a man truly become man. For in seeing his Creator man catches a glimpse of what he was intended to be. He who would see his God would then see the reason for death and the purpose of time. Destiny? Tomorrow? Truth? All are questions within the reach of the man who knows his source. It is in seeing Jesus that man sees his Source.

—Max Lucado, *God Came Near /*
Chronicles of the Christ

The mirror says a lot! Very few people walk out of their homes on their way to a job or an outside activity without first looking in the mirror. My own family (mainly men) would probably attest to the fact that I personally spend more time in front of one than they do! The mirror is a valuable item for showing flaws, and it helps us make sure a section of hair is not out of place or that our colors match. Have you ever returned to the workplace after lunch just to find out hours later upon leaving that a piece of spinach was lodged in your front teeth or a drop of mustard was on your white blouse—but not one person pointed it out to you? In the rush to return promptly, you failed to take one last look in the mirror. Speaking for myself, I appreciate the gentle touch of the hand that tucks the tag on the back of my sweater back inside where it belongs or discreetly lets me know I have my skirt tucked inside my pantyhose. One quick look in the mirror surely would have made a difference!

As we have studied together the fruit of the Spirit and adorned the white dress of salvation with an accessory that represents each one, it's now time to take a look in the mirror. Yes, the mirror shows only the outward results of our adorning. It is my prayer that each of us has grasped the wonderful fact that love, joy, peace, long-suffering, gentleness, goodness, meekness, faith, and temperance stem from the Spirit, who is at work within each believer. They are a picture of the Father, revealed to us by His Son, Jesus, and should be evident in our lives under the control and power of the Holy Spirit. When we look in the mirror of God's Word, whom do we see? What do we see? In John 14:7, Jesus says, "If ye had known me, ye should have known my Father also; and from henceforth ye know Him, and have seen Him." In the crowd was Philip. He said in response to Jesus's statement that if He (Jesus) would show him and those with him in the crowd the Father, it would be totally sufficient for them.

Now, if we are honest with ourselves and those around us, haven't we been the same way? Can we recount the times that the Lord has provided in a way that seemed hard to explain? Perhaps He even answered a prayer that was heavy on our hearts and lifted the heavy burden. There may even have been other times when we wondered if He was aware of the present need or burden. I'm guilty! When I spend time daily in His Word and seek His face, I've found my faith to be strengthened to a point that it would seem that nothing—I mean *nothing*—would cause me to waver from whom I know Jesus to be in my life. It was the same with Philip, only Jesus was trying to prepare those who walked close by His side for the day when He would no longer be with them on earth. He had just told them earlier, "I go to prepare a place for you" (John 14:2). I think I know how Philip must have felt when Jesus asked him this searing question, "Have I been so long time with you, and yet hast thou not known me, Philip? He that hath seen me hath seen the Father; and how sayest thou then, Show us the Father?" (John 14:9).

I've been saved about forty-eight years now, and I've heard the Lord through His Spirit ask me some pretty searing questions as I've spent time in His Word. But this is the process by which we become more like Him. Remember the story that took place on the afternoon of Easter, involving two people walking on the road of Emmaus? One of the two is identified as Cleopas, and the second person may very well have been his wife. They were in deep discussion about the recent events in Jerusalem when they were joined by the risen Lord. Read Luke 24 when you have your next quiet time and ask the Holy Spirit to be your Teacher as you do so. Jesus joined them in their walk and asked why they were so sad. Verse 16 says, "But their eyes were holden that they should not know him." Cleopas's reply was pretty matter-of-fact in assuming Jesus to be a stranger who was totally unaware of the latest happenings. He began filling this stranger's ears with all that had taken place at the hands of the chief priests and rulers and then capped it off with a statement revealing personal doubts as to whether or not the one crucified was "he which should have redeemed Israel" (verse 21). They had also heard that the women who appeared at the sepulcher in the wee hours of the morning had witnessed a missing body. To get their story straight, they sent others to confirm all that the women reported as true. Jesus, still engaging in their conversation, took the time to remind them of the teaching of Moses and why

Christ came. As they approached the city, their interest piqued to the point that they wanted Him to stay and eat with them. It wasn't until Jesus broke the bread, blessed it, and then proceeded to hand it to them that they realized who it was that had joined them. All of a sudden, they recalled how their hearts burned and were stirred within them when He began teaching them from the scriptures. Why, it moved them to the point where they could do nothing else but make their way back to Jerusalem to search out the other eleven disciples. Boy, did they have a story to tell now!

I like what the devotion in John Stott's *Through the Bible, Through the Year* had to say:

> Notice what Luke tells us about their eyes. According to verse 16, their eyes were kept from recognizing him; according to verse 31, their eyes were opened and they recognized him. The question is, what happened to make the difference? And how can our eyes be opened as theirs were? Firstly, we know Christ through the Scriptures. Jesus reproved them for being so slow to believe the prophets, and then he took them through the three main divisions of the Old Testament—the Law, the Prophets, and the Psalms (v. 44), explaining their teachings about the sufferings and glory of the Messiah. As Jesus said earlier, "The Scriptures...bear witness to me" (John 5:39 RSV). So we need to look for Christ in all the Scriptures. As we do, our hearts will burn within us. Secondly, we can know Christ through the breaking of bread. It was then their eyes were opened and they knew him. Here then, are two major ways by which Cleopas and his companion came to recognize

the risen Lord, and by which we may know him today — through the Scriptures and through the breaking of bread; through the Word and the sacrament.

The Word of God is our mirror through which we can see God. Jesus came to teach us the things of the Father and spoke only of the Father. Colossians 1:15 tells us He (Christ) is the image of the invisible God. We can only know God because of the death, burial, and resurrection of Jesus Christ. We can only know Christ as we look to the scriptures and by faith trust His work at Calvary to be the God-approved payment for our sins.

During the writing of this chapter, I started reading *The Jesus I Never Knew* by Phillip Yancey. The title alone intrigued me. The writer spoke of his own personal preconceptions of the Jesus he had known since childhood through flannel-graph lessons to the Jesus portrayed in the Gospels — having the sincere desire to relate it all to the world in which we presently live. He wanted to convey to the reader that the Jesus we all think we know so well was, is, and continues to be the central figure of history. He said, "The Jesus I got to know in writing this book is very different from the Jesus I learned about in Sunday School. In some ways He is more comforting; in some ways more terrifying." As I continue to read God's Word and the accounts of Matthew, Mark, Luke, John, Paul, and all the other Holy Spirit-inspired writers, I can relate to that statement! Yancey goes on to say,

And yet I am not writing a book about Jesus because he is a great man who changed history. I am not tempted to write about Julius Caesar or the Chinese emperor who built the Great Wall. I am drawn to Jesus, irresistibly, because he positioned himself as the dividing point of life — my life. "I tell you, whoever acknowledges me before men, the Son of Man will also acknowledge him before the angels of God," he said. According to Jesus, what I think about Him and how I respond will determine my destiny for all eternity.

The perfect Son of God experienced thirst physically, but during His encounter with a Samaritan woman who was making her way to a watering well (and of whom he asked for water to quench that thirst) He offered *her* spiritual water. Although she saw him as a weary traveler in need of something from her, she was about to learn about *His* living water. She had her own questions to ask this stranger, but realized in the end that the perpetual and eternal satisfaction she received from Him could not compare to the temporary satisfaction of the physical. Read it yourself in John 4. "Jesus answered and said unto her, Whosoever drinketh of this water shall thirst again; But whosoever drinketh of the water that I shall give him shall never thirst" (John 4:13–14).

Jesus was born in a lowly manger in a smelly stall, while sinful men occupied the last available room in a more comfortable place. God chose a simple virgin with great faith to carry him to term. Her simple reply was, "I am the Lord's servant" while present-day abortions take place because inconveniences or other reasons take priority. He victoriously defeated Satan in the desert during a time of fasting and alone time with his Father. I really love this statement by Phillip Yancey regarding this ordeal: "Although Satan posed the tests, in the end it was he who flunked them. In two tests he merely asked Jesus to prove himself; by the third he was demanding worship — something God would never accede to. The Temptation unmasked Satan, while God remained masked." Jesus always cut to the heart of the matter, and it didn't matter to whom He was speaking. His ultimate purpose in His life, His miracles, His teaching, and His death was to draw all people to the Father.

When we look in the mirror, we see someone made in the image of God! When we give our life to Him, His desire is that we be conformed to the image of God day by day—through stumbles and accomplishments alike. The Christian walk is not easy, but then neither was the life of the Son of God. He came to die. He cares that much for us. He was misunderstood, misquoted, spat upon, and crucified.

> For even hereunto were ye called: because Christ also suffered for us, leaving us an example, that ye should follow in his steps: Who did not sin, neither was guile found in his mouth: Who, when he was reviled, reviled not again; when he suffered, he threatened not; but committed himself to him that judgeth righteously. (1 Peter 2:21–23)

We can mirror the fruit of the Spirit. Are you having trouble loving someone right now? Let Christ love that person through you. Are you struggling to live a life of joy with everything caving in on you right now? Let the joy of the Lord be your strength. Are you stressed out and lacking peace? Allow Jesus to speak peace to you where you are. Is the illness or situation you are experiencing taking its long, drawn-out toll on you? Let the suffering Savior take your hand and be long-suffering with you. Do you want to just plunge headlong out of an unbearable relationship that seems irreconcilable? Let the gentle Savior give you the response that may be the turning point for reconciliation.

Is there someone who could benefit from the resources God has so abundantly put into your hand? Go and give cheerfully in the name of Jesus. Has God placed a call on your life to which you haven't given your whole heart?

By faith commit to Him afresh and anew in obedience, remembering His promise to complete it until the day of Jesus Christ. Are you critical of someone who has fallen from the faith? Did you hold this person in high esteem, but now you've written him or her off because he or she has let you down? Let Jesus go with you to that person and in meekness bring him or her back to the arms of the Savior. Are you letting fleshly desires affect your witness to those around you? Open yourself up to the temperate hand of God and allow Him to teach you self-control. It's a choice — your choice! This is what Jesus looks like — and so much more!

Anyone who knows me also knows I love the old hymns of the faith. Quite frankly, I don't even know why we call them old because their message is just as relevant today as it was when they were written. One of my favorites, in particular, is "Oh to Be Like Thee," by Thomas O. Chisholm. Allow me to bless you with the words.

> Oh, to be like Thee, blessed Redeemer,
> This is my constant longing and prayer;
> Gladly I'll forfeit all of earth's treasures,
> Jesus, Thy perfect likeness to wear.
>
> Chorus:
> Oh! to be like Thee, Oh! To be like Thee,
> Blessed Redeemer, pure as Thou art;
> Come in Thy sweetness, come in Thy fullness;
> Stamp Thine own image deep on my heart.

Oh! to be like Thee, full of compassion,
Loving, forgiving, tender and kind.
Helping the helpless, cheering the fainting,
Seeking the wandering sinner to find.

Oh! to be like Thee, lowly in Spirit,
Holy and harmless, patient and brave;
Meekly enduring cruel reproaches,
Willing to suffer, others to save.

Oh! to be like Thee, Lord, I am coming,
Now to receive the anointing divine;
All that I am and have I am bringing,
Lord, from this moment all shall be Thine.

Oh! to be like Thee, while I am pleading,
Pour out Thy Spirit, fill with Thy love,
Make me a temple meet for Thy dwelling,
Fit me for life and heaven above.

Prayer

Lord Jesus, I confess today that the more I see who You are as revealed in Your Word, the more I don't know You. I want to be like Jesus! I want others to see Jesus in me! Just as You humbled Yourself in obedience to the Father, it is my desire to do the same. Thank You for Your Word, which shows me the things of the Father, for it's there I claim Your promises and realize "I can do all things through Christ who strengthens me." I want to always remember that with You I can do absolutely anything. Remind me when I forget. My desire is to be like Jesus, and it's in His Name I pray. Amen.

CHAPTER 12

Walking in the Spirit

Stand fast therefore in the liberty wherewith Christ hath made us free, and be not entangled again with the yoke of bondage.

—Galatians 5:1

This I say then, walk in the Spirit, and ye shall not fulfill the lusts of the flesh. For the flesh lusteth against the Spirit, and the Spirit against the flesh; and these are contrary the one to the other, so that ye cannot do the things that ye would. But if ye be led of the Spirit, ye are not under the law.

—Galatians 5:16–17

While I was praying over the final chapter and the completion of this book, Johnny and I celebrated thirty-five years in the ministry of evangelism. With one hundred guests in attendance, we reminisced about all the events that have taken place since our days at Bible college and the amazing people with whom the Lord has blessed our lives and who also played a huge part in allowing us this milestone. There were lean days when it took every last dime to get us to a meeting (sometimes using every available means of transportation to do so!) and days of fatness when we witnessed God's provision in abundance.

We also remember the years when our children were young and I would stay home with them while Johnny did weeklong crusades. It was during these times that anything that could go wrong did, but we witnessed the provision and protection of the Lord through it all! There was a mutual sense of resolve that this was what the Lord had called us to and we would do it until Jesus called us home to heaven or we witnessed His return. And we're not done! I hope we can have another thirty-five years! We just don't know. What we *do* know is that we serve an awesome God, who began the work, and we trust Him to finish it. Like Paul, our desire is to stay faithful in running the race and to hear the Lord say, "Well done, good and faithful servant."

There can be a stick-to-itiveness that is embedded deep down within the believer — no matter where the Lord has called him or her in service to Him. It is the Holy Spirit that nurtures it as we respond to Him. It is maintained by knowing how to walk in the Spirit each and every hour of the day, every day of the week, and every month of the year — with every passing year. Are we doing everything perfectly and without flaws? No, indeed! Were there temptations to choose another path where there was more security in areas of finances or job employment? Yes! In and of themselves, none of these are wrong. Under the guidance of the Holy Spirit and the calling He placed on our lives, our desire was to do what was *best*. In the case of Johnny and me, it was (and is) *resolve* — not *resources*! We walk by faith.

Paul begins the fifth chapter of Galatians with the imperative to stand fast — or better still — keep on standing!

We are the children of the King! We are children of promise! It was made possible through the shed blood of Jesus, and thanks to the cross of Christ, *it is possible*! Salvation is free to all people, but we shouldn't forget that it came at a high cost. Striving to keep the law is a noble gesture, but Paul points out the end result of futility that comes when we realize the impossibility of keeping the whole law. We get entangled with "dos" and "don'ts" and sooner or later will even come up with a few laws of our own to compensate for those already written (which is exactly what the Jews did). Lest we get too pious, we also do the same.

Jesus is the perfect example of God's ideal. But what about "Be perfect, therefore, as your heavenly Father is perfect" (Matthew 5:48)? When we read the verses prior to the list of the fruit of the Spirit in regard to the works of the flesh, do we stop to realize that this is who we are except by the grace of God? I, like Paul, must admit that "in my flesh dwells no good thing." No, we may not be murderers. We haven't taken another life. Yet we read that "Whosoever hateth his brother is a murderer; and ye know that no murderer hath eternal life abiding in him" (1 John 3:15). One can be blissfully married to the same woman for many years, but do we take into account what Jesus said in Matthew 5:28, "But I say unto you, that whosoever looketh on a woman to lust after her committeth adultery with her already in his heart"?

That list in Galatians 5:19–21 is a full description of who we are apart from Christ, and it is ugly and fully describes every one of us! Oh, how I love what Phillip Yancey said in his book *The Jesus I Never Knew*: "Grace is for the desperate, the needy, the broken, those who cannot make it on their own. Grace is for all of us. We CANNOT follow any of God's precepts without it! Yet, we don't have to live a life of despair over our own failure to be perfect, even though that's what we're commanded to be. But, we should never stop striving!" Yancey focused on the Sermon on the Mount as just one example of the tragedies that come when we take God's ideals and turn them into forms of legalism. How ashamed we should be to demand that people cut their hair or change their clothes to become a Christian! None of us could get clean enough to receive God's wonderful gift of salvation. Yancey goes on to say,

> ...the worst tragedy would be to turn the Sermon on the Mount into another form of legalism; it should rather put an end to all legalism. Legalism, like the Pharisees' will always fail, not because it is too strict but because it is not strict enough. Thunderously, inarguably, the Sermon on the Mount proves that before God we all stand on level ground: murderers and temper-throwers, adulterers and lusters, thieves and coveters. We are all desperate, and that is in fact the only state appropriate to a human being who wants to know God. Having fallen from the absolute Ideal, we have nowhere to land but in the safety net of absolute grace.

I just love it when someone else so eloquently says what I often struggle to say myself!

There is a sweet and wonderful ministry of the Holy Spirit in the lives of believers! It's hard to walk in the Spirit—but even harder if we are ignorant of His works. I reread the notes on "The Doctrine of the Holy Spirit" by Dr. Harold Willmington in *Great Truths from God's Word* (Systematic Theology) and would like to share the opening statement:

> During one of his missionary trips, the Apostle Paul questioned a group of Ephesian "church

members" (actually they were disciples of John the Baptist) about the doctrine of the Holy Spirit. Their answer must have shocked him somewhat, for they replied, "We have not so much as heard whether there be any Holy Ghost" (Acts 19:2). If Paul was shocked, surely the Father and Son were saddened as they viewed yet another example of the almost universal ignorance concerning the ministry of the blessed third Person in the Trinity. This statement by these Ephesian disciples, perhaps as no other in the Bible, illustrates the sorry and shameful treatment often given Him. His very existence has been ignored and His ministry misunderstood.

From this teaching and the study of the Bible, what we cannot ignore is the fact that the Holy Spirit is a person, just as much as the Father and the Son, Jesus, are. The details of His ministry throughout scripture as He resides within every believer; guiding, anointing, convicting, interceding, protecting, clothing the saints of God, and filling them with power (to name only a few) are just the beginning of my own personal quest to know Him and His work in my life. It is the Spirit who teaches me to become more and more like the Savior.

Even as a young believer, I remember how He dealt with me when I willfully took my own route instead of yielding to His guidance. I recall one particular birthday close to the end of a high school year. Wanting to celebrate this special day, my friends and I decided it would be cool to skip the remaining classes and head to a nearby gathering place to have some innocent fun. We did it with great ease and success! All was good until I made it back to school in time to catch the bus for the long ride home.

We lived far from town. It only took a few minutes for the sickening feeling in my gut to take over. So began the reasoning and war within. Here are a few of my thoughts of reason at that moment: I made good grades. Very rarely did I even miss school altogether. My friends and I didn't get into any mischief, which would result in someone calling my parents to voice a complaint. I didn't think my teachers were even concerned over my absence from class. Then began the "what-ifs": What if they were? What if a call had already been made? What if someone saw me without my knowledge and secretly ratted me out? Even if I did somehow get by with all this, how would I feel about myself in regard to my relationship with the Lord? Now, that was the zinger! It had been not too long since I had memorized Hebrews 11:6 and claimed it as my life verse. It says, "But without faith it is impossible to please Him…" Was this pleasing to the Lord? The Holy Spirit was making it quite clear that a deception had taken place and I was the ringleader in its inception. I was also doing a pretty good job in manipulating its concealment. There was only one thing to do, and it involved coming clean. Firstly, I asked for forgiveness from the Lord on that hot bus seat and was ready to take the heat from whatever means my folks would use to drive the hard lesson home to me. The temptation to back down arose once face-to-face time with my mom was there, but the desire to please the Lord in all this was the motivating factor to follow through.

My point is this: I remember how it felt deep down inside my being. I was fully aware of the Spirit's conviction during the process. I wish I could say that this was the only incident since, but it would not be true. My prayer is that I'll *always* be sensitive to the Spirit's voice and not grow numb to His loving conviction. This is what God's Word teaches as *a Spirit of discernment.*

We have some wonderful liberties that are ours. They have taken the place of the life of bondage we once knew as unbelievers. As Christians, we can also still be enslaved if we fail to obey that sweet, small voice. It's difficult to walk after the Spirit if we don't know what the Bible teaches us concerning His ministry in our lives. His voice is deafened when we repeatedly go our own way, and we grieve Him. We are summoned to a life of daily dying to self and the old person so that the life of Christ reigns supreme. In *The Believer's Secret of Holiness* by Andrew Murray, this is what he says regarding our new life in Christ:

> This life is not like the life of nature, a blind unconscious principle, involuntarily working toward its object in unresisting obedience to the law of its being. This life is the Spirit of life in Christ Jesus—the Spirit of holiness—the Holy Spirit dwelling in us and leading us into the fellowship of the living Christ. We must accept death to the flesh and death to self with it willing and working as the birthplace of our experience of the power of the Spirit of holiness. In each struggle with sin, in each exercise of faith or prayer, we must enter into the death of Jesus and the death of self.

Romans 6:14 says, "For sin shall not have dominion over you; for ye are not under the law, but under grace."

John the Baptist, the forerunner of Christ, said, "He must increase, but I must decrease" (John 3:30). Christ has delivered us from the enslavement of sin. Murray went on to say this regarding slavery:

> In olden times when the Turks or Moors often made slaves of Christians, large sums were

frequently paid to ransom those who were in bondage. But it happened more than once that the ransomed ones, far in the interior of the slave country, never received the news; the masters were only too glad to keep it from them. Others received the word, but had grown too accustomed to their bondage to rouse themselves for the effort of reaching the coast. Slothfulness or hopelessness kept them in slavery. They could not believe that they would ever be able to reach the land of liberty in safety. The ransom had been paid. In truth they were free, but by reason of ignorance or want of courage, in actuality they remained in bondage.

"Where the Spirit of the Lord is, there is liberty" (2 Corinthians 3:17). He has defeated sin and death. By faith, we are no longer under the curse of sin! Yes, we still live in sin's presence, but we now are temples of the Holy Spirit, who gives us power over sin! We need to ever strive to be the women of God who are adorned with the fruit of the Spirit. "And they that are Christ's have crucified the flesh with the affections and lusts. If we live in the Spirit, let us also walk in the Spirit" (Galatians 5:24–25).

Like adorning a dress with jewelry and accessories, so the sweet Holy Spirit longs to adorn our lives with Christ's own likeness. We should be taking off the old and putting on the new with a heart that longs to be like Him. Join me in committing this final verse to memory. May you experience the love, joy, peace, long-suffering, gentleness, goodness, faith, meekness, and temperance and no longer desire the vainglory that comes from the lust of the flesh, the lust of the eyes, and the pride of life. "I will greatly rejoice in the Lord, my soul shall be joyful in my God; for He hath clothed me with the garments of salvation, he hath covered me with the robe of righteousness" (Isaiah 61:10). May you be adorned with the fruit of the Spirit and walk in His power today and always!

Prayer

Lord Jesus, thank You for your great salvation and the life of freedom that comes when I give You full reign. Thank You for the life of grace that I've received from You and can now offer others. Forgive me when I choose bondage over the wonderful liberty with which You have made me free. May Your righteousness be a joy and strength to me as by faith I serve You in obeying Your will. Clothe me in Your righteousness. My desire is to daily walk in the Spirit and be ever sensitive to His sweet voice as He directs my life. In the Name of Jesus I pray. Amen.

REFERENCES

1. A. B. Simpson, *Walking in the Spirit* (Waxkeep Publishing, 2013).
2. Oswald Chambers, *My Utmost for His Highest* (Journal), Uhrichsville, OH: Barbour Publishing, Inc.
3. *Esther: It's Tough Being a Woman*, a study on Esther by Beth Moore (Nashville, TN: Lifeway Publishing, Inc., 2008).
4. *Give Me This Mountain*, an autobiography by Helen Roseveare (London: InterVarsity Press, 1966).
5. John Stott, *Through the Bible, Through the Year: Daily Reflections from Genesis to Revelation* (Grand Rapids, MI: Baker Books, 2006).
6. W. Phillip Keller, *A Shepherd Looks at Psalm 23* (Grand Rapids, MI: Zondervan Publishing House, 2007).
7. Dr. James Dobson, *When God Doesn't Make Sense* (Wheaton, IL: Tyndale House Publishers, Inc., 1993).
8. Osbeck, Kenneth, *Amazing Grace: 366 Inspiring Hymn Stories for Daily Devotions* (Kregel Publications, 1990), "O to Be Like Thee," 255.
9. Max Lucado, *God Came Near/Chronicles of the Christ* (Sisters, OR: Multnomah Publishers, Inc., 1986).

10. Phillip Yancey, *The Jesus I Never Knew* (Grand Rapids, MI: Zondervan Publishing House, 1995).

11. Dr. Harold L. Willmington, copyright. *Great Truths from God's Word* (Forest. VA: Systematic Theology, 2003).

12. Andrew Murray, *The Believer's Secret of Holiness*, Classic Devotional Studies (Minneapolis, MN: Bethany House Publishers, 1984).

Printed in the United States
By Bookmasters